LATER
ANGLO-SAXON ENGLAND
Life & Landscape

To Sarah and Jake

LATER
ANGLO-SAXON ENGLAND
Life & Landscape

Andrew Reynolds

TEMPUS

First published 1999
First paperback edition 2002

PUBLISHED IN THE UNITED KINGDOM BY:
Tempus Publishing Ltd
The Mill, Brimscombe Port
Stroud, Gloucestershire GL5 2QG
www.tempus-publishing.com

PUBLISHED IN THE UNITED STATES OF AMERICA BY:
Tempus Publishing Inc.
2A Cumberland Street
Charleston, SC 29401
www.tempuspublishing.com

British Library Cataloguing in Publication Data.
A catalogue record for this book is available from the British Library.

ISBN 0 7524 2513 7

Typesetting and origination by Tempus Publishing.
PRINTED AND BOUND IN GREAT BRITAIN.

Contents

Ordeal
Punishment
Execution sites

List of illustrations

Text figures

Colour plates

Preface and Acknowledgements

This book was prepared at the invitation of Peter Kemmis Betty whose efforts and patience have been appreciated through the process of moving house twice and the arrival of a child. The need for a synthesis of recent and not-so recent work into the landscape of later Anglo-Saxon England was felt necessary for two main reasons. My teaching at the Institute of Archaeology brought about the realisation that there was no single source written from an archaeological perspective that encompassed such aspects of later Anglo-Saxon society as governance and administration and civil defence, together with traditional themes such as rural settlement and urban development. Urban studies in particular have remained vibrant over the last twenty years or so and their treatment here aims to provide only a brief overview. Archaeology has revealed many new rural settlements of our period and so there is a rather extended treatment of this material. The book claims to be neither fully comprehensive nor in full agreement with the prevailing views of individual specialists. Rather, a balanced view is attempted with reference to key debates and sites.

Friends and colleagues prior to publication read various chapters, although it goes without saying that any remaining inaccuracies or idiosyncrasies are the responsibility of the writer. For commenting on earlier drafts I am grateful to John Blair and Paul Stamper. The fine reconstruction drawings were ably produced by Sarah Semple, whilst all of the line drawings were produced with great clarity and consistency by Alex Langlands with the assistance of James Conolly. Helen Geake, Chris Loveluck, Mark Gardiner and Duncan Brown provided illustrative material, often at short notice, whereas Henry Escudero prepared the black and white plates for publication.

The Research Committee at the Institute of Archaeology in London made a generous grant for preparation of the illustrations.

The book itself was written in fits and starts in Oxford, but also in Wormelow, Herefordshire thanks to the generosity of Birgitta Jansson.

A volume without specific references to the published work of others is a difficult thing to write for one trained in academic modes of composition. I have, therefore, attempted to mention by name at least some of those archaeologists and historians upon whose labours much of the material included in this book is derived. Inevitably, there will be omissions, but an acknowledgement is made to the fact that the volume of scholarship encompassed here is but a fraction of that which exists. For their help in various ways over the last 18 months, I should like to thank in particular James Graham-Campbell, Alexander Deacon and Simon Roffey. By far the biggest burden has befallen my partner Sarah Semple, who has suffered the late nights and unorthodox lifestyle of one immersed in writing.

1 *Location of principal sites mentioned in text*

Introduction:
sources and approaches

Take by night, before it dawns, four turfs from the four corners of the plot, and make a note of where they belonged. Then take oil and honey and yeast, and milk from each beast that is on the land, and a portion of each type of tree that is growing on the land, apart from the harder woods, and a portion of each nameable plant, excepting buck-bean only, and then apply holy water and let it drip thrice on the underside of the turfs and say then these words: grow, and multiply, and fill the earth.

So runs the opening part of an Old English remedy for unfruitful land, the so-called *æcerbot* charm of the early eleventh century. Without the reference to holy water, this passage might be accepted as a clear description of some pagan ritual enacted by farmers worshipping their deities in the hope of successful yields. That it is not, however, for the instructions given in the charm require the parish priest to enact part of the ritual. The charm may well have roots in pre-Christian folk magic, but it does help to introduce the reader to a world where things were very different from our own. It can be tempting to romanticise the past, to see the Anglo-Saxon period as a predominantly heroic age of literary and artistic achievement, but the farmers participating in fertility rituals were very likely placing great faith in their effectiveness, for their livelihoods depended on the productivity of the land.

Anglo-Saxon England was a violent place for some, an oppressive place for most, and a world of extravagance and wealth for the very few. This book attempts to provide an introduction to the settlements and landscapes experienced by the Anglo-Saxons using primarily the evidence from archaeological excavations.

The English landscape contains a considerable wealth of features left to us by the Anglo-Saxons, whose physical remains can still be seen today if armed with the right approaches. One of the principal aims of this book, therefore, is to introduce the reader to the various approaches taken by modern academics and field archaeologists working on Anglo-Saxon England.

Most village and town names are derived from Old English, the position of settlements in the landscape were largely fixed by the time of the Norman Conquest, whilst the system of shires, in southern England at least, has its origins in the eighth and ninth centuries. The web of agricultural estates of the late Anglo-Saxon period is largely tangible today in the form of ecclesiastical parishes and, by accident of survival, there are indications that many of our rural parish churches were in existence by this time. Despite the fact that the Normans planted many new towns in the landscape in the course of the twelfth century, a large number of modern urban centres have their origins in the Anglo-Saxon period, either as royal or religious centres or as places of refuge and defence.

The network of routes of communication in the English landscape is the result of developments dating back to pre-Roman times, but the Anglo-Saxons were responsible for many of our modern roads, both major and minor. In fact, it is the English landscape which exhibits the most tangible traces of our Anglo-Saxon past in ways which, as this book attempts to show, are accessible to all who look in the right places.

The study of England in the centuries prior to the Norman Conquest is a rewarding pursuit, contrary to the long-held popular perception of the period as the 'Dark Ages'. The jewellery of the period is amongst the finest produced by any culture in the world, whilst the Anglo-Saxon literary and artistic achievements present an almost unparalleled record in intellectual and creative terms. The visually stunning survivals and discoveries from the period represent, of course, the material aspirations of the elite classes: kings and their counsellors, and the inhabitants of monasteries — with often little distinction between the two in terms of pedigree. The lives of the greater mass of the population are reconstructed through rather less exotic remains, but, when gathered together, the results of archaeological and historical enquiry reveal complex social groupings with an intimate knowledge of how to best exploit their surroundings.

Students of Anglo-Saxon history and archaeology are fortunate in that they can observe a wide range of social and economic phenomena during the years 700–1100. By about 700 the conversion of the English to Christianity was well under way and kings of varying influence ruled over increasingly clearly defined territories. From the seventh century onward, the landscape became steadily more organised and efficiently exploited and this is reflected in the settlement archaeology of Anglo-Saxon England. As the period progresses, there is clear evidence for the development of specialised settlements, a highly organised system of public administration and justice and a highly regularised monetary economy. In the countryside, the need to meet the demands of taxation ensured that the subsistence farming economies of the earliest post-Roman centuries developed into communal surplus-producing industries by the time of the Norman conquest. Certain marketing and religious centres and places of defence and refuge grew into exceptional settlements, that we now call towns.

If one adopts the widest possible perspective on Anglo-Saxon archaeology, then its value for examining developments in other cultures at other periods becomes apparent. The growth of the complex society in existence by the Norman Conquest occurred over a period of some 500 years following the gradual emergence of archaeologically and historically visible elites from the sixth century. By the time of the Norman Conquest in 1066, Anglo-Saxon England had become a sophisticated nation state with a developed social culture, which was in many ways little changed by the Conquest. The Anglo-Saxon period, therefore, bore witness to many of the central themes and issues studied by archaeologists and historians throughout the world.

The fact that the archaeological record of Anglo-Saxon England is paralleled, if not always accurately mirrored, by documentary sources allows archaeological discoveries to be examined against a historical narrative. When the various biases of the historical record are considered and balanced against the evidence from archaeological discovery, it is possible to build theoretical archaeological scenarios based upon the observed archaeological manifestation of historical events or processes. Archaeologists can then examine sites that display distinctive physical characteristics but which lack specific documentation, and suggest pathways of interpretation.

Although Anglo-Saxon society has left a substantial impression on the present landscape, there is often a tendency to overemphasise continuity of institutions and places or to seek the earliest origins for features only clearly observed in later times. English landscape history is no exception. In the recent past scholars were concerned to find the earliest roots possible for aspects of English life and culture. The origins of open field agriculture, for example, were attributed to Germanic migrants of the fifth and sixth centuries. Moreover, in the 1970s, a number of scholars argued that rural estates had passed through the Late Romano-British/migration period horizon and on into the medieval period with little alteration to their original form.

To a certain extent the 'continuity' view could be said to reflect a continuous pattern of emphasising, or creating, ties to the past. Certainly, our Anglo-Saxon predecessors were masters of creation when it came to matters of dynastic origin and, later, the ownership of land and the contractual obligations of land transactions. It is only by a critical and detailed analysis of the documentary record and archaeological evidence that we can begin to assemble a more feasible history of the Anglo-Saxons. It is worth noting, however, that forgery and exaggeration in historical accounts are of interest in themselves, as they help to illuminate the political and economic power games of the Anglo-Saxon elite. The earlier Anglo-Saxon kings, eager to legitimise their claims to authority, created semi-mythical lists of descent, or genealogies. In the later Anglo-Saxon period, claims to tracts of land purportedly granted centuries earlier were disputed by the more powerful Anglo-Saxon monasteries, such as Winchester Old Minster, on the basis of their own forged charters.

The traditional view of the English landscape as a quiet, sedentary preserve must now be firmly dismissed in the light of advances in archaeological research and discovery. This book, therefore, attempts to chart the increasing social and economic complexity observable in the development of England between the seventh and eleventh centuries.

The scope of this book

The chapters in this book are organised on a thematic basis to allow readers to 'dip in' to particular topics; the chapters themselves are structured so as to provide a broad chronological overview of each theme. All too often, books based primarily upon the evidence afforded by archaeology assume a detailed understanding on the reader's part of modern archaeological method and theory, both of which are continually being developed and refined by academics and field archaeologists world-wide. Whilst this volume makes no claims to furnish the reader with a history of archaeological thought and method, a short introductory section is included which describes how archaeologists reach the conclusions and interpretations upon which this book is founded.

Similarly, the problems associated with documentary sources are outlined, albeit briefly. Contemporary written records are utilised in this book to provide information where archaeology is silent or problematic, or to illustrate situations where archaeology either compares or contrasts with the traditional historical narrative. Contrary to popular belief, the written sources of the period are not all concerned with the careers of bishops and kings, and battles. There exists a rich and varied body of literature, written largely without the political and ideological bias which affects any reading of the various 'lives' and calendrical annals. These sources have much to offer and they are used throughout the book.

Anglo-Saxon England has been traditionally defined, using documentary sources, as beginning in the early decades of the fifth century, with the arrival of Germanic migrants, and ending at the moment of the Norman Conquest of 1066. Whatever the fate of the indigenous Romano-Britons, there is no evidence of them quitting the country, either through voluntary migration or via 'ethnic cleansing'. Similarly, people did not demolish their 'Anglo-Saxon' houses in favour of 'Norman' ones, nor smash their pots or change their dress fashions in response to military domination. The chronological scope of this book, therefore, is rather less precise in its definition than one written from a solely historical perspective.

The starting point of the book is the seventh century. Whilst much has been written in recent years about the two centuries immediately following the end of Roman Britain, the same cannot be said of the following centuries, at least not from an archaeological perspective. Archaeological scholarship, in common with other academic disciplines, tends to advance in fits and starts following periods of stasis dominated either by a single prevailing view or by the development of so-called 'schools' of thought. The archaeology of Anglo-Saxon England during the period 700-1100 has seen major advances over the last 35 years in particular, within the various specialised fields which contribute to the advancement of the subject. The motivation for this book therefore, comes from the need to combine the results of various specialist studies into a single condensed account of current thinking about the later Anglo-Saxons. While it is the intention to flag-up most of the major on-going discussions in Anglo-Saxon archaeology, in general a balanced view is attempted throughout. There will always be a necessity in books such as this to sweep rather broadly over the intricacies of current debate, but the section on further reading at the end of this volume will allow readers to pursue additional themes and case studies of their choice.

There are certain topics, central to Anglo-Saxon England, that are beyond the scope of this volume. No attempt is made to provide a running political history, and the architecture and history of the Anglo-Saxon church is left out beyond the most general social and economic considerations. Cemetery location is considered in its landscape context, but the intimate details of specific burial rites are not explored. Neither is this volume concerned with art history or the minutiae of object classification. Instead, this book is offered as an introductory guide to town and country and to the daily circumstances and experiences of the people of Anglo-Saxon England.

Many of the better-known sites are either discussed or at least mentioned, but similarly, many are not. One could not hope, even if it were desirable, to cover every category of site

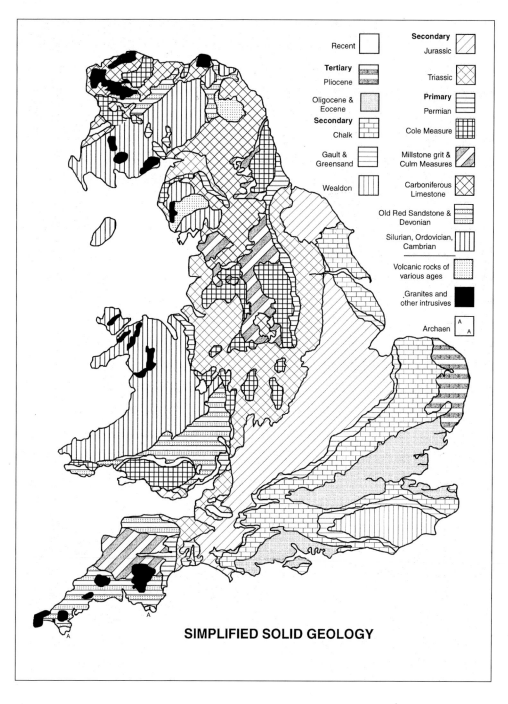

		Secondary	
Recent		Jurassic	
Tertiary			
Pliocene		Triassic	
Oligocene & Eocene		**Primary**	
Secondary		Permian	
Chalk		Cole Measure	
Gault & Greensand		Millstone grit & Culm Measures	
Wealdon		Carboniferous Limestone	
		Old Red Sandstone & Devonian	
		Silurian, Ordovician, Cambrian	
		Volcanic rocks of various ages	
		Granites and other intrusives	
		Archaen	

SIMPLIFIED SOLID GEOLOGY

2 *Geology of southern Britain*

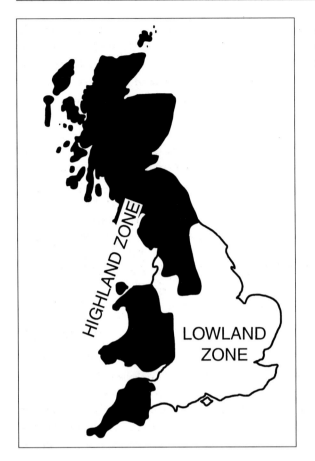

3 *Highland and lowland zones in the British Isles.* Redrawn from Hill 1981

or artefact in anything but the most substantial of volumes. Both well-known and lesser-known excavations are presented in sufficient numbers to give a representative view of particular aspects of the period such as high-status residences or rural settlements.

Chapter 1 sets the scene with a summary of the fifth and sixth centuries, and a more detailed account of England in the seventh century. Chapter 2 considers the development and terminology of social hierarchies, with a consideration of the roles and duties from the slave class through to the responsibilities of kings with regard to the governance of their subjects. Chapter 3 provides an account of the administrative structure of Anglo-Saxon England from the level of kingdoms down to governance in the localities. Chapters 4 and 5 explore the evidence for settlement and economy in rural and urban contexts. The book concludes with a brief postscript assessing the impact of the Norman Conquest in cultural terms.

Regional variation

The English landscape is characterised by considerable geographical and topographical variation. Such strong regional and intra-regional contrasts have ensured varying responses by human populations to the landscape in which they live. In very general terms, England may be considered in terms of highland or upland areas, usually comprising the oldest geological formations, and lowlands, formed of younger, sedimentary rocks or glacial deposits (**2 & 3**). Highland areas are commonly viewed as marginal areas, although they are often found to support specialised farming communities — probably through necessity rather than choice. The highland areas of England include the Peak District and the Pennines in the north with Dartmoor, Exmoor and Bodmin Moor in the south-west.

The lowlands have traditionally supported the larger share of past populations and the Anglo-Saxon period proves no exception to this. Indeed, the difficulties of transport and communications compounded with the restricted productivity of highland areas has led to the now long-held consensus view of the uplands as politically and economically marginal land in the post-Roman period. England, however, is a small country by comparison to its contemporary continental counterparts and this factor of scale must always be borne in mind when considering regional variation. Although bleak uplands are characteristic of certain regions, their relative extent is not considerable. The basic natural resources necessary to sustain human settlement are not far to hand in any region and it is only the highest, most inhospitable areas that were avoided by hill farming communities.

A network of waterways, exploited for the necessities of daily life on the one hand and for local and regional communication and transport on the other, traverses both upland and lowland England. It is clear from a range of sources that waterborne transport was both cheaper and faster than overland means of communication, but roads, nevertheless, played an important part in the development of trade and the movement of armies among other more local functions. Topographical considerations determine the usefulness of waterways for communication and in upland areas the seasonal nature of many watercourses has had a direct effect on the nature of settlement and land use. Similarly, the course of overland communication in upland areas is often likely to be determined by local topography, in contrast to lowland regions where highways could be laid out far more efficiently. Local micro-topographical variation can be observed to influence routeways of local economic significance, especially at the boundaries between lowlands or vales and uplands where pastoral farming has introduced the need for drove-roads from river valley to upland pasture. The chalk downland landscapes of Sussex, Hampshire, Bedfordshire, Berkshire and Wiltshire provide particularly fine examples of such routes.

Besides geological differences in landscape, there are vegetation contrasts, but these are often difficult to reconstruct for any particular point in the past. An important problem that faces landscape historians is the reconstruction of the extent of woodland in Anglo-Saxon England, although attempts have been made (**4**). Certain regions, such as the Weald of Sussex and Kent, and parts of Berkshire, are known from place-name and documentary evidence to have been densely wooded during the Anglo-Saxon period. It is frequently difficult, however, to be sure of the precise chronology of landscape development, and Anglo-Saxon archaeologists have much to learn from prehistorians who, in recent years, have revealed the dynamism of the earliest stages of the development of the English landscape. A prime example of the misunderstanding of English landscape history is

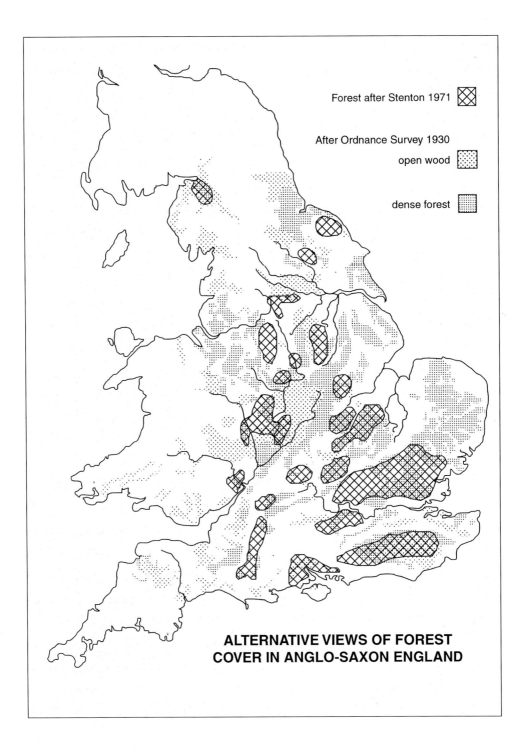

Forest after Stenton 1971

After Ordnance Survey 1930

open wood

dense forest

ALTERNATIVE VIEWS OF FOREST COVER IN ANGLO-SAXON ENGLAND

4 *The possible extent of woodland in Anglo-Saxon England.* Redrawn from Hill 1981

5 *Rectilinear fields overlain by the Roman Pye Road in south Norfolk.* Redrawn from Williamson 1988

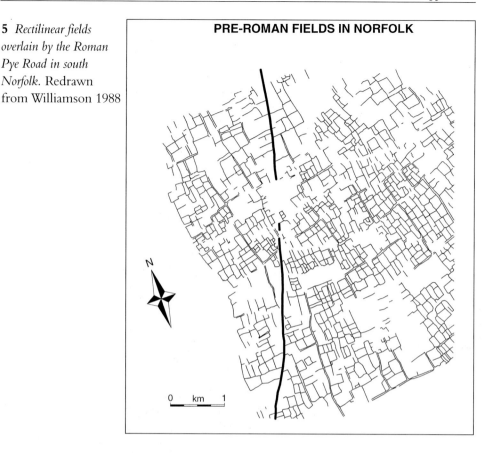

PRE-ROMAN FIELDS IN NORFOLK

provided by the now-refuted concept of 'ancient' woodland. Until relatively recently it was considered by many that tracts of primeval woodland existed which had survived millennia of human modification of the landscape. Such a view of long-term conservatism is now no longer upheld and scholars broadly agree that no part of England lay untouched by human interference beyond the earlier Iron Age (*c.*600BC) at the very latest.

Given that the English landscape has been continually remodelled since at least the early Neolithic period (from the fifth millennium BC), it is clear that succeeding populations settled and worked a landscape etched with the boundaries, monuments and agricultural features of their predecessors. This is an important point because period-specific studies are often written as though the landscape was a blank sheet of paper prior to the commencement of the author's particular period of interest. In fact, it has been clearly shown through detailed local and regional studies that patterns of land division observed in the later Middle Ages or even up to the present day were originally set out at a much earlier date. Within this scenario there exists the further complication that different regions have experienced different chronologies of alteration by the human hand. For example, the Dengie Peninsula of Essex and parts of the lower slopes of the South Downs in central Sussex have been interpreted as the result of Roman country planning, or *centuriation*, where regular blocks of fields were laid out as part of a large-scale re-organisation of landscape. Similarly, on Dartmoor the work of Andrew Fleming has demonstrated that large-scale cohesive field-systems, laid out in the Later Bronze Age, could determine, in part, the layout of later fields. In south Norfolk, Tom Williamson has argued for the substantial survival of pre-Roman co-axial, or rectilinear, blocks of fields (**5**) that, by default, would have characterised the landscape in the Anglo-Saxon period. On the Berkshire Downs, Della Hooke has observed an Anglo-Saxon estate boundary that precisely follows the boundaries of a set of small rectangular fields of possible Roman origin subsequently overlain by medieval ridge and furrow fields.

Richard Bradley has coined the term cohesive to describe such formally determined field-systems, whereas less regular field-systems, seemingly the result of piecemeal addition to what we might call small-holdings, are termed agglomerated according to Bradley's scheme. Agglomerated field-systems are commonly found on upland landscapes, where they may be attributable to any period from the Early Bronze Age (*c*.2000 BC) up to recent times. Landscape historians have made much of the fact that there is no characteristic 'Saxon' type of field prior to the earliest 'open fields' familiar to students of the medieval period. It is now clear, however, that the Anglo-Saxons most commonly utilised long established field patterns, at least until the tenth century, although relict field systems still remain in certain regions.

Despite the fact that many of the field boundaries extant in the early medieval landscape were of earlier origin, it is the exploitation and productivity of fields that is of principal concern to early medieval archaeologists along with the desire to reconstruct patterns of agricultural estates. Clearly, the survival of field boundaries from earlier periods does not imply continuity of cultivation or of pastoral farming into the early medieval period and we must be prepared to allow for periods of abandonment. To a certain extent, the evidence provided by pollen deposited in various natural catchment zones, such as the often deeply stratified deposits in dry valleys, can allow for a reconstruction of landscape history. Much more 'environmental archaeology', as it termed, is needed before any national picture can be drawn. The study of early medieval boundaries and landscapes plays an important role in medieval archaeology and the more important case studies are considered in Chapter 3.

In Anglo-Saxon England, regions with valuable mineral resources served areas where these were lacking. In general, Anglo-Saxon exploitation of natural resources was similar in range to that of the Roman period with many of the regions continuing to produce minerals on a nationally important scale until the nineteenth or even the twentieth century. Cornwall is well known for its tin production and the Mendip Hills in Somerset for lead, whereas the sinuous band of Jurassic limestone that stretches from the West Country to Lincolnshire provided high-quality stone for ecclesiastical buildings and sculpture. Although the British Isles contain a wealth of natural materials, certain types of non-indigenous stone, such as Niedermendig and Mayen lava for querns and precious and semi-precious stones for jewellery, were imported from the continent and beyond.

As a final general point, the close proximity of England to a range of continental neighbours must always be borne in mind. For many years, archaeological interpretations of cultural developments in England were based on what is known as the 'Invasion Hypothesis'. Prehistorians attempting to account for cultural change by means of incoming populations, gradually came to accept that the mechanisms involved in the exchange of ideas are likely to be far more varied. Anglo-Saxon archaeology now incorporates a variety of perspectives on the relationship between England and the continent and, indeed, it has been the foremost discipline in advancing our knowledge of international trade and trading settlements of the period. Although continental peoples including Franks, Germans and Scandinavians undoubtedly did have influence upon material culture, housing, art and architectural styles in England between the fifth and eleventh centuries, movements of people, objects and ideas occurred on a two-way basis. English exports included books, ornamental metalwork, missionaries and slaves amongst less exotic commodities such as grain and wool, but a much broader range of social relationships between the English and their continental neighbours is probable.

Traditional period divisions and the nature of the evidence

Scholars of Anglo-Saxon England are broadly agreed that the period between the departure of the Romans and the arrival of the Normans can be divided into three roughly equal blocks, based upon social and economic change: Early Anglo-Saxon England *c*.450-*c*.650; Middle Anglo-Saxon England *c*.650-850; and Late Anglo-Saxon England, from *c*.850-1066. Instead of using the label Anglo-Saxon, which has various cultural and ethnic connotations, many archaeologists now use the term 'early medieval' to cover the entire period from the decline of Roman authority up to the later eleventh century.

The archaeology of Early Anglo-Saxon England is characterised by furnished inhumation and cremation cemeteries and small farmsteads. In contrast to the burial sites, where social scales appear to become better defined during the fifth and sixth centuries, settlements display little trace of a social hierarchy until the seventh century. The evidence of dress fashions from excavated burials suggests that loosely defined fifth-century communities developed regional identities during the sixth century. It is not until the seventh century, however, that high-status settlements and extraordinarily wealthy burials are found which provide tangible details about the nature of early kingship. The conversion of the English to Christianity during the course of the seventh century defines the beginning of the Middle Anglo-Saxon period. After a period of some two hundred years, during which the church became firmly rooted in the English landscape, the height of Viking raiding, followed by settlement, brought about major social changes that define a mid-ninth-century threshold between Middle and Late Anglo-Saxon England.

From the ninth to the eleventh centuries, England developed into a sophisticated nation state comprising an amalgamation of earlier kingdoms. Trouble with the Vikings continued after a short period of peace in the late ninth and early tenth centuries and they finally conquered England, in the guise of the Normans, at the Battle of Hastings in 1066. Archaeologists feel increasingly uncomfortable about using the Norman Conquest of 1066 as a defining moment in cultural terms, however, as the archaeological record offers only very partial support for this view. In cultural terms the end of Anglo-Saxon England can be placed variously between 1100 and 1200, depending on whether one is looking at, for example, timber or masonry architecture, towns, ceramics or metalwork, amongst other aspects of the period.

Finding archaeological sites of the Anglo-Saxon period is notoriously difficult. There are still regions that are almost devoid of evidence for Anglo-Saxon settlements, particularly those of the Middle Anglo-Saxon period. Early Anglo-Saxon archaeology was, until recently, almost entirely dependant on the evidence of cemeteries, whilst Middle Anglo-Saxon archaeology has been transformed in the last twenty years by the discovery of urban places, industrial sites and rural settlements which, until this time, were desperately little-known. Church architecture survives in varying degrees in over four-hundred buildings of Middle and Late Anglo-Saxon date, with some impressive examples such as the eighth- or ninth-century church at Brixworth in Northamptonshire and the Late Anglo-Saxon chapel of St Lawrence at Bradford-on-Avon in Wiltshire.

The archaeology of Middle and Late Anglo-Saxon burial customs is presently a hotly-debated subject, especially since the recognition that the seventh-century conversion of the pagan English to Christianity was less influential upon burial practices than had once been assumed. Whilst enclosed Christian cemeteries are known from the seventh century, it seems that they only became widespread during the tenth and eleventh centuries, when changes in the structure of landholding brought with it the foundation of a considerable number of our parish churches.

Since the end of the Second World War, the redevelopment of England's historic city centres has revolutionised our understanding of urban development after the departure of the Romans. Urban locations present exciting possibilities owing to the quality and quantity of information that can be extracted from deep sequences of human occupation. Urban origins lie in the Middle Anglo-Saxon period and the study of the growth of towns is well served by archaeology to the end of the Late Anglo-Saxon period and beyond.

The massive increase in the number of excavations in rural locations in the 1970s led to a second explosion in the quantity and, just as significantly, the quality of excavations of Anglo-Saxon rural settlements. There are very few survivals of settlement earthworks dateable to before *c.*1000 and they are still a rarity before *c.*1100. The majority of Anglo-Saxon sites, therefore, are discovered by chance during archaeological excavations concerned at the outset with other periods. The effects of later ploughing or settlement redevelopment have successfully erased the surface traces of the majority of Anglo-Saxon settlements and so other archaeological techniques are required.

High-status rural settlements of Middle Anglo-Saxon date have been successfully located, although in small numbers, since the 1950s by using aerial photographs. Lower status rural settlements however, tend to be found unexpectedly or identified by chance finds. Geophysical surveying, which includes the techniques of resistivity, magnetometry and magnetic susceptibility, is often used to follow up a discovery from aerial photographs or stray finds.

Archaeology

Archaeological excavations and chance finds provide the raw materials for the reconstruction of daily life before the Norman Conquest. The most tangible remains come from settlements and from burial sites, although in recent years archaeologists have become increasingly aware of the importance of viewing such remains in relation to each other. Using the information provided by archaeological excavation in combination with finds of individual objects, it is possible to examine the development of particular territories or regions. This approach to the study of the past is termed 'landscape archaeology'. Indeed, landscape archaeology is now the principal approach to studies of the past and this is particularly the case in Anglo-Saxon archaeology now that the broad outlines of artefact typologies are established. Artefact based studies are of course vital, as they provide the chronological frameworks upon which any assessment of social and economic development must be based. The construction of elaborate series of developmental sequences of particular artefact types, such as brooches, beads, dress-fittings and vessels of various kinds, provide the basis for dating archaeological sites. Whilst there has been a tendency to ascribe changes in artefact types and art styles to social change, archaeologists now realise the limitations of such narrowly focused approaches to the period.

Overall, there has been a tremendous bias towards the study of Early Anglo-Saxon archaeology, particularly the rich pagan cemeteries of the period. Although this situation has been criticised in recent years, it has ensured that research into the pagan English is now a highly advanced discipline.

In general terms, archaeologists use the data from excavations to reconstruct both daily life and the social climate within which populations lived and worked. The material finds from excavations can be interpreted as status indicators and, when assemblages from different excavations are compared, a hierarchy of sites might be observed. Alternatively, comparisons of finds assemblages might reveal specialisation within individual groups who inhabit a locality or region. In Anglo-Saxon England both social scenarios can be observed.

There is always a danger when attempting to use assemblages from archaeological sites that under-representation of certain categories of materials can affect the way that we view the nature of occupation or land-use. Organic finds, such as leather shoes, wooden bowls and spoons and textiles, are rare finds from excavations. Only in damp or waterlogged circumstances will such objects survive.

Despite the situation that they are frequently subject to aggressive corrosion, metals are always likely to be poorly represented on archaeological sites. Metal objects could be reworked when broken, or rapidly superseded by the arrival or innovation of a new style or type. Accordingly, the range of artefacts represented by the average assemblage is a poor indicator of the consumption of iron and copper or base metal alloy in the past. Iron was used in a wide variety of structural applications including locks and keys, door fittings, nails and staples as well as for other everyday items such as knives, pins, tools and dress accessories. Copper alloys were used largely for dress items including belt fittings and brooches, although other objects such as horse furniture and high-status artefacts such as censers for use in churches are also found. Base metals were used in the late Anglo-Saxon period to produce cheap, mass-produced badges and brooches for sale in urban markets. Objects of copper and lead alloy are rare finds, although they are frequently decorated, often in styles whose period of currency is known from independent sources.

Although metal objects are usually rare, the fact that they were so commonly reworked is of benefit to the archaeologist owing to the fact that reliable typological sequences of stylistic development have been established for everyday objects such as horseshoes, arrowheads and knives. The more exotic metal objects, particularly those of precious metals or copper alloys, are likely to have remained in circulation longer than utilitarian objects and so their use as dating tools is more restricted, although still of value. In fact, it is the metal finds from excavations that often provide the most reliable dates, as local pottery styles are commonly not dateable to within a century or more.

Ceramic artefacts are plentiful on most archaeological sites, although regional variation in both production and consumption ensures that identified Anglo-Saxon settlements are thin on the ground in certain regions. Again, this does not reflect a pattern of settlement that once existed, but an archaeological problem of site recognition. Traditionally, archaeologists have used pottery for the purpose of providing a dated sequence of observable changes in the forms of individual pots and in the variability of assemblages as a whole. By studying the pottery from rich and deeply stratified deposits, it can be possible not only to examine changes in the forms of pots over time, but also the popularity of certain products by way of comparison between the longevity and quantity of each ceramic type.

During post-excavation analyses, ceramics are divided by specialists into groups defined by fabric (the physical characteristics of the fired clay). Raw clay dug straight from the ground is unsuitable for potting and requires preparation. Usually a coarse temper is added to the clay, which improves the workability and firing of the product. Tempers are most commonly derived from geological series in close proximity to the potter's workshops. In the downland areas of Wiltshire, Berkshire and Sussex, for example, late Anglo-Saxon pottery is frequently characterised by tempers of flint and chalk, whilst potters working in the sand and clay vales adjacent to downland areas often used sand. The amount of temper added varies according to the requirements of the potter, but it is nevertheless frequently possible to establish its provenance. Studies of the provenance of potting clays and their tempers allow archaeologists to reconstruct patterns of production and trade on a local, regional, national and international basis.

Once the pottery from an excavation has been divided on the basis of its physical characteristics, the range of vessel types produced in each fabric is established. It might, for example, be observed that a wide range of cooking pots is produced in a coarse fabric whilst tableware such as jugs and platters are made using finely-tempered clays. In general, coarse pots are far more common from excavations than fine pots, whilst international imports are usually restricted to coastal ports and high-status sites where the consumption of rare commodities took place as part of the process of emphasising social hierarchies. In Anglo-Saxon England international imports are found almost entirely in coastal towns and on monastic sites, although there are a few exceptions and these are considered later.

Further categories of finds from archaeological excavations are the remains of plants and animals, often termed 'ecofacts'. Such materials have their own particular problems of survival and interpretation. It is important to establish when looking at plant remains how the deposits in which they were found came to be formed as very small plant remains, such as seeds, can be carried to lower layers by natural processes. Archaeologists call the study of site formation processes 'taphonomy'. Animal bones too, suffer from problems of representation owing to the fact that certain parts of animals are suitable for making particular objects such as combs and pins. Scavenging animals are also likely to have affected the quantity of bones found on archaeological sites, although not in such a highly selective way.

There are differences too, between different types of sites with regard to the range and quantity of the artefacts and ecofacts recovered from excavations. Patterns of rubbish disposal in towns contrasted markedly with those in the countryside. Domestic waste generated by urban dwellers was normally dumped in pits within the confines of individual properties, whereas rural communities tended to pile up their rubbish, forming what archaeologists term middens, before carting it out into the fields for use as manure. We have already noted that certain types of artefacts are more commonly represented than others from excavated sites and also the fact that some objects remain in circulation for much longer periods than others. With these factors in mind, archaeologists divide the deposits found on excavations into three types: primary, secondary and tertiary.

Primary rubbish is generated at the place where it is discarded and represents a direct archaeological trace of a discreet episode or event. As a parallel, chopping down a tree and leaving the waste where it lay constitutes a primary deposit. Moving a waste product from its point of origin to another location forms secondary rubbish. During such processes only part of the initial deposit of waste is likely be moved. For example, a cooking pot dropped on the floor of a house will produce both primary waste — tiny sherds of broken pottery, that may lay hidden — and secondary waste — larger sherds taken from the house and thrown into a pit or onto a midden. Tertiary waste is produced when a midden is spread over cultivated ground or when an infilled rubbish pit is cut into by activity in a subsequent period. In both cases the result is a mixture of artefacts from different periods but found together in the same layer.

The reader need not assume at this point that the problems of taphonomy are insurmountable as archaeologists now use measured critical approaches to identify and understand problems of site formation processes. It is hoped that this short consideration gives at least an introduction to how archaeological evidence can be understood but also an adequate explanation for the archaeologists concern about the find-spot, or 'context' of artefacts. Whilst an artefact sold in the sale room might have art historical or technological interest its significance will always be reduced without secure knowledge of its context.

The evidence from archaeological excavations is a precious and valuable thing and we would do well to remember that an archaeological site is a document that can 'only be read once in its original form'.

Documentary sources: prose texts

Overall, it can be fairly stated that English documents from the before the Norman Conquest present an unparalleled record in both quality and breadth when compared to contemporary north-west European survivals. The prose texts are largely the records of daily life and experiences; they are the Old English equivalent of modern house deeds, collections of legal cases, minutes of meetings, wills and letters. Between them they throw light both intentionally and unintentionally on most aspects of the daily situation in early England.

The prose texts are generally accepted as reliable in their portrayal of daily life and realistic in their illumination of official procedure of church and state. The sources can be broken down according to the function of the documents. Laws, sometimes known as dooms after the Latin *domus*, were issued by English kings from the time of Æthelberht (580x93–616x18) until the reign of Cnut (1016–35). They comprise lists of a wide range of offences with details of the appropriate fines to be paid to the king, church or other injured party. Prior to Patrick Wormald's studies, however, there has been a tendency to use the laws with little regard to the chronological development of legal practice that can be discerned. Besides prescribing settlements and punishments for various wrongs, the laws also provide insights into the daily workings of the Anglo-Saxon judicial system. The laws of the tenth-century kings describe in some detail the workings of local courts, the raising of posses and the ritual of judicial ordeal among other processes. The legal texts are referenced throughout this book where they relate to the daily situation or to other phenomena where an archaeological dimension is apparent.

There is a range of further texts that frequently contain useful information about rights and circumstances, folk beliefs and social intercourse. Short official letters, or writs, were first used as a mode of communicating the wishes of the king to the localities, at least from the time of Alfred (871–99), although it is only from the late tenth century onward that the evidence permits a detailed understanding of public administration. There is an extensive series of Late Anglo-Saxon writs, largely dating from the reign of Edward the Confessor (1042–1065) and these often relate to ecclesiastical estates. Writs commonly take the form of a brief greeting from the king, followed by some instructions, usually confirmation of obligations and rights. The writs, therefore, can provide information about the status and role of particular estates. The earliest surviving communication written in English is a letter sent by Bishop Waldhere of London to Berhtwald, Archbishop of Canterbury in 704 or 705. Letters, however, were to remain very much the preserve of the clergy and the highest of state officials including the king.

Perhaps the most important documentary sources for the Anglo-Saxon period are Bede's *Ecclesiastical History* and *The Anglo-Saxon Chronicle*. Bede was a Northumbrian monk whose home monastery was the great seventh-century foundation at Jarrow, and he is commonly referred to as the 'father of English history', owing to his extraordinary pursuit of reliable source material for his works. Bede's *History* was completed in 731 and it is the most important work regarding the early history of the English, particularly the process of the conversion to Christianity. *The Anglo-Saxon Chronicle* exists in several versions of varying chronological coverage, although, in common with Bede's *History*, the accuracy of the earlier entries is questionable. In the case of the *Chronicle*, events recorded after about the middle of the ninth century are likely to be largely reliably reported, but the further back in time one looks the deeper one becomes immersed in the imagination and political bias of the scribe. Indeed, the *Chronicle* appears to have been assembled during the ninth century and in a West Saxon context to judge by its flattering treatment of that royal house and its achievements. The *Chronicle* entries run into the twelfth century, but the principal value of the source is its description of the political scene of the Late Anglo-Saxon period, most notably the social upheaval caused by the Viking incursions from the end of the eighth century onward.

Domesday Book represents one of the most impressive administrative achievements of the post-Roman period. The *Anglo-Saxon Chronicle* under the year 1085 records how William the Conqueror 'held a very deep speech with his wise men about the land, how it was held, and with what men'. The surviving survey covers most of England with assessments of the value of each vill, or estate, in 1066 and 1086. Overall, some 13,418 vills are named. The survey itself was carried out by groups of commissioners who compiled their information on a shire by shire basis.

Domesday Book allows us to reconstruct the extent of royal landholding at the time of the Norman Conquest, although we are fortunate to have a series of wills detailing estates in possession of the West Saxon royal house from the time of King Alfred and, later, of King Eadred (946–55). Alfred's will details royal holdings spread over a wide area of southern England, but also gives details about the sums of money left to his children (£1000 to his sons and £500 to his daughters) and to his ealdormen (100 *mancuses*). A range of further financial gifts is listed, but an attempt to keep the royal estates intact is made by Alfred's insistence that the directions in his father King Æthelwulf's (839–58), will be observed to the best of the ability of the new landlords.

Further documents describe donations of land and relics to monastic houses from royal and ecclesiastical bequests, whilst the world of the rural peasant and his master is portrayed in two documents known as estate memoranda dating to the end of the Anglo-Saxon period. A whole range of sermons, particularly of the latter part of our period, give an insight into the moral concerns expressed by the leading churchmen of the day. Wulfstan, Archbishop of York (1002–23), for example, drafted his famous *Semo Lupi ad Anglos*, or 'sermon of the wolf to the English', in addition to much of the legislation of both Æthelred (979–1016) and Cnut and at least 21 other homilies.

On a more domestic level, an important source for charms and medicinal practice is provided by a tenth-century Winchester manuscript known as *Bald's Leechbook*. The book describes treatments for ailments running from shingles to spider bites, and from hair-loss to over-virility. Perhaps the most important source for landscape reconstruction, however, is Anglo-Saxon charters, especially those that contain boundary surveys.

Anglo-Saxon charters

Anglo-Saxon charters are documents that record the conveyance of land or rights, usually from the king to the church but also to private individuals. Scholars of the nineteenth and early twentieth centuries explored the charters primarily for the information that they provide about political circumstances. Charters were attested by both secular and ecclesiastical figures of high rank. The observed pecking order of names in these so-called witness lists has enabled historians to explore aspects of early social structure, politics and governance. Of principal interest to archaeologists are the land charters. Grants of land most commonly comprise three parts; a preamble which gives an account of who is granting the land or rights and to whom; a list of witnesses, in order of importance, and in many cases a written description of the boundaries of the estate in question.

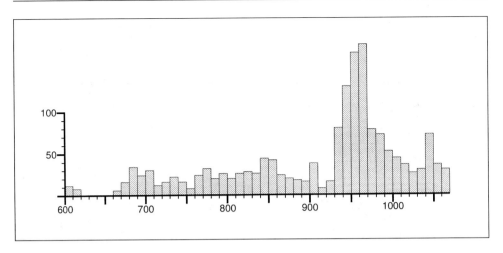

6 *Distribution by decades of Anglo-Saxon charters with bounds.* Redrawn from Hill 1981

The first section was written in Latin, whereas the boundary clauses were almost always produced in the vernacular; Old English. The earliest known land grants are from the seventh-century kingdom of Kent, but these and other early charters did not as a rule contain boundary clauses. There is some dispute as to the date of origin of grants by royal charter. The majority of scholars see the introduction of charters as a later seventh-century phenomenon attributable to the archiepiscopate of Theodore (668–90), whilst others have argued that the few charters of the early seventh century are authentic. Charter studies are a highly specialised field, and disagreements about the dating and authenticity of individual documents are frequent concerns amongst those working on the material.

Archaeologists working on boundary clauses must be conversant with such issues, particularly as a large proportion of the eighth- and ninth- century grants of land only had boundary surveys added to them in the tenth or eleventh centuries. After a moderate increase in the number of surviving charters over the period from the seventh to the ninth century, there was an explosion in the number of grants made in the middle decades of the tenth century (**6**). Although it might be argued that charters of a later date are more likely to survive, there are good reasons for accepting the trends shown by the surviving corpus. The tenth-century proliferation of land grants is directly linked to contemporary changes in the way that the countryside was organised, and this is explored in Chapter 3.

Charter bounds are of the greatest interest to archaeologists as they provide contemporary descriptions of estates which, in most cases, can be identified in the modern landscape (**7**). Anyone who has traced a set of Old English bounds on the ground cannot fail to experience genuine excitement at the realisation that so much of the Anglo-Saxon countryside still remains visible in a tangible form. The results of many years of research into the landscape context of the bounds have allowed a number of general observations to be made. Della Hooke has noted that boundary clauses run clockwise as a rule and tend

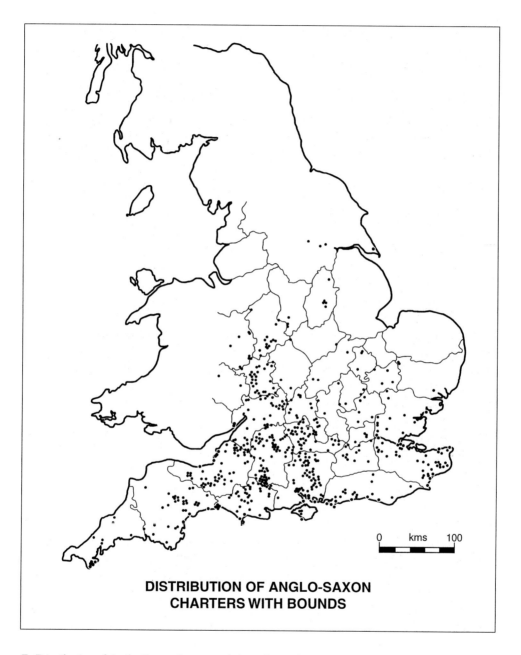

**DISTRIBUTION OF ANGLO-SAXON
CHARTERS WITH BOUNDS**

0   kms   100

7 *Distribution of Anglo-Saxon charters with bounds.* Redrawn from Hill 1981 after Goodier unpublished

to start at one corner of an estate, although others are known where the description begins midway along one of the sides.

The language and choice of landmarks recorded in the boundary clauses is that of the recording of a mental map of an estate. The setting down in writing of what was most likely a commonly remembered set of directions, did not entail any unit of measurement, but instead features of the landscape served as markers. Natural features such as trees, watercourses and rocks, were commonly incorporated in estate bounds along with burial sites, outlying agricultural settlements and roads of varying types as well as a whole host of agricultural features.

Documentary sources: poetry

The study of Old English literature is a long-established and highly-refined discipline that encompasses the skills of the palaeographer, the etymologist and the historian, amongst others. Whilst the context of much of the Old English literary corpus is well understood, the dating of individual pieces is a matter of intense debate and there is little indication that there will ever be agreement with regard to certain poems, including the great epic *Beowulf*.

In fact, *Beowulf* serves as an exemplar. The poem survives in a single manuscript of about AD1000 known as *Cotton Vitellius Aiii*; the first part of the name refers to Sir Robert Cotton (1571–1631), whose great collection of Old English documents formed part of the initial holdings of the British Museum in 1753. Many documents from the Cotton collection were lost after a fire at Ashburnham House in 1731, but very fortunately the only known copy of *Beowulf* was one of the survivors. *Beowulf* is the best known of the Old English poetic corpus and arguably one of the most stunning pieces of English literature. The tale of the high-status barrow burial of the poem's hero has long been recognised to belong, in origin, to the age of Sutton Hoo and warrior kings, as outlined below in Chapter 1, and for many years an eighth-century date has been broadly accepted for its composition. Recently, however, American scholars in particular have begun to question an early date for the *Beowulf* poem with some suggesting that the piece need not be earlier than the eleventh century. Whatever the date of composition, there are strong grounds for accepting an early basis, at least for certain aspects of the poem. The Old English poem *The Battle of Maldon* recalls the outcome of a battle between the English and the Vikings in 991 in a style strongly reminiscent of an earlier heroic age, and this point serves to illustrate but one of the difficulties with the dating of the *Beowulf* poem.

As with virtually all of the poetic material, the details of contemporary relevance often require teasing out from a mass of earlier folk traditions and Christian textual and illustrative imagery, which are often found combined in individual pieces. Illuminated manuscripts present problems when it comes to establishing just how much contemporary culture the artist has incorporated in his drawings. Many, if not most, of the known corpus of manuscript illustrations and illuminations take as their exemplars continental manuscripts often of a much earlier date. Martin Carver, however, has shown how a careful comparison between exemplar and copy can allow contemporary artefacts to be identified.

Place-names

Our final source of evidence under consideration is that of place-names. A properly trained linguist is able to distinguish the various subtleties exhibited by modern spellings of words in order to establish their Old English forerunners. In certain cases developments of language have obscured the original meaning of place-names. In addition, our earliest record of many settlement names is Domesday Book which itself represents the culmination of a long period of name-attribution, name-change and name-loss in the landscape. Consequently, it can be difficult to establish with any degree of confidence a refined chronological view of landscape development based upon place-names alone. It is possible to examine the range of place-names recorded in the earliest historical narratives such as Bede's *Ecclesiastical History*, but it still remains a difficult issue to establish when a place-name was first applied and for how long its literal meaning was relevant. The survival of place-names containing British words suggests an earlier origin within the period for those names, as they imply verbal communication between speakers of both British and Germanic languages.

Place-names do, however, allow general patterns of settlement to be explored. Settlement names are frequently related to their topographical context, and an adequate explanation for many village names will often be found by observing the lie of the surrounding land. The original agricultural function of many rural settlements is recorded in their modern names, whilst English rivers often preserve their British names. The plotting of distributions of different classes of place-names can aid their understanding within a broader historical context. The Scandinavian place-names of the north and east are a good example of this approach where the distribution of Scandinavian names broadly agrees with what is recorded in the *Anglo-Saxon Chronicle* with regard to Viking settlement in the British Isles.

Besides throwing light on rural settlement and economic patterns, the place-name record also preserves memories of superstitious associations with certain landscape features. Work by Sarah Semple has shown how certain earthworks of an origin unknown to the Anglo-Saxons were often associated with malevolent entities and generally regarded with fear and trepidation. Such features include linear banks and ditches as well as Bronze Age barrows with names implying a perceived ghoulish presence. Besides the names of settlements, or 'major names', there exists a vast number of 'minor names' applied to individual fields or landscape features. Our earliest source for field names within a given parish is usually a mid-nineteenth-century Tithe Apportionment with accompanying map. The study of minor names can allow elements of past landscapes to be reconstructed, including arable fields and woodland, as well as the sites of mills, quarries and lost settlements.

Archaeology and history

A fundamental issue, which relates to medieval archaeology as a whole, is the relationship between history and archaeology. The arrival of literacy with the Christian church at the close of the sixth century ultimately led to an increasingly documented society. The construction of detailed historical narratives, such as the *Anglo-Saxon Chronicle* and Bede's *Ecclesiastical History*, provided the pioneers of Anglo-Saxon archaeology with a chronology of events. The dates of early battles, people and places were often taken at face value and linked to discoveries of archaeological material in an uncritical manner. The Sutton Hoo Mound 1 ship burial discussed in Chapter 1 is perhaps the most well-known example of an attempt to establish a link between an archaeological deposit and an historically documented figure.

The nature of the historical sources is outlined above, but it is necessary here to emphasise the considerable difficulties of directly linking the two sources of evidence. In fact, the only circumstance under which the two sources can be tied together is when inscriptions that mention documented individuals are recovered from archaeological excavations or are found as part of standing structures, or when an archaeological site or structure can be related to highly specific documentation. Even in such cases as these, the attribution of a precise historical date to the archaeological deposit in which the inscription is found depends on whether the find is *in situ* (literally, in its original place).

Inscriptions in the Anglo-Saxon period are either in Old English or Latin and are found largely on items of metalwork or on stone sculpture and an example of each is presented below to illustrate varying archaeological usefulness according to context. The famous Alfred Jewel, housed in the Ashmolean Museum in Oxford, is one of the finest survivals of ninth-century craftsmanship in gold, enamel and rock crystal. The object is believed to be the body of a pointer, or reading aid, and bears the inscription AELFRED MEC HEHT GEWYRCAN, or, 'Alfred ordered me to be made'. The superior quality of the find in relation to the inscription, is accepted by most as sufficient reason to link the object with King Alfred. Sir David Wilson, however, has noted the lack of any royal title in the inscription, a surprising omission at a time when they were of great significance. Clearly, an association with Alfred would allow the art styles on the object to be assigned to the period of his life. Despite good circumstantial evidence, however, it is impossible to be certain about the link between artefact and individual. This factor becomes significant in the study of early medieval art history, as the subject relies on all too few accurate dates for artistic developments, and thus it is relevant to archaeologists who use decorated artefacts as dating evidence

An example of a thoroughly reliable, and very remarkable, inscription can be found at Kirkdale in North Yorkshire. Here, an Anglo-Saxon sundial, set above the south door is inscribed 'Orm, the son of Gamal, bought St Gregory's church when it was broken and fallen, and had it made anew from the ground in honour of Christ and St Gregory, in the days of Edward the king and Tosti the earl'. Tosti was the brother of King Harold (king, January to October 1066), the last of the Anglo-Saxon kings, and a powerful earl from 1055 to 1065 according to the *Anglo-Saxon Chronicle*. If the inscription is an integral part of the nave of the present church, its reference to Tosti's earldom allows the architectural characteristics of the church to be independently dated; the mention of an earlier ruinous church at Kirkdale has recently been borne out by archaeological enquiry, which has also questioned the context of the sundial.

Anglo-Saxon studies have become increasingly multi-disciplinary over the past two decades. The long-established fields of art history and constitutional history have been joined by geography, English, palaeography, onomastics (place-names), and last but certainly not least, archaeology. Archaeology has immeasurably advanced our knowledge of life in early England and, instead of being seen as a source for 'filling the gaps', now allows us to question aspects of the historical record.

1 England in the seventh century and the early Anglo-Saxons

Introduction

England by 700 was a very different country from that found by the earliest Germanic settlers who had arrived in apparently increasing numbers from the early fifth century. Although the country is named from one of these migrant peoples, the *Anglii* from the Angeln region of North Germany, archaeologists have begun to doubt the extent to which folk movement took place. Instead of warriors invading *en masse*, many scholars now take a rather less aggressive view of events. Indeed, some have argued that the cultural changes observable in fifth-century England can be explained in a variety of ways without resorting to the so-called 'invasion hypothesis'.

The extent to which Britons still occupied the landscape in the early fifth century is difficult to determine. There is evidence, however, that gives an indication of at least a persistent scatter of British settlements. Many of the names of watercourses in England are of British and not Old English origin. This is in complete contrast to settlement names, of which the vast majority are of Old English derivation. Settlements of British origin are indicated by the incorporation of the Old English word *weala*, meaning foreigner, in the place-name. Common examples of these types of names include Walton and Walcot, although both Wales and Cornwall contain *weala* and show that the term could apply equally to territories as to individual settlements. The survival of British names for landscape features and for habitation sites can only indicate direct contact between Briton and Saxon in certain regions, with the Britons retaining their identity living in discrete settlements.

In the earlier days of the study of Anglo-Saxon archaeology, it was believed that invading Germanic groups had literally driven the native inhabitants of Britain westward into Wales and the south-west as well as across the English Channel where the British 'refugees' settled in and gave their name to Brittany. This view was supported by the paucity of sites that showed evidence of occupation in the earlier fifth century. The development of archaeological field techniques and refinements of dating methods have subsequently led to identification of many more sites of fifth-century date, although these largely fall into two separate groups. On the one hand there is the evidence for continued occupation within Roman towns, on the other are new settlements and burial sites which exhibit a Germanic character either by the nature of their structural remains or by the presence of decorated metalwork of continental type.

The identification of fifth-century settlements is largely hampered by the difficulties of assigning a fifth-century date to the deposits found. In fact, it is often difficult enough to assign an early or even mid-fifth-century date to burials that contain early types of decorated objects. Nevertheless, the appearance of a new and highly distinctive material culture occurred during the fifth century and with it began an upward turn in social and economic organisation. Before we consider the remains of the earliest settlements and cemeteries of Germanic character, however, the nature of the evidence for continuity deserves some attention.

The end of Roman Britain

It has long been recognised that occupation in certain urban centres continued after Britain became separated from the Roman Empire early in the fifth century. The traditional date for the end of Roman Britain is 410 when the Emperor Honorius sent a letter to the *civitates* (districts) of Britain telling them to defend themselves. There has been a tendency to overemphasise the nature of life in former Roman urban centres, but some probably continued to serve a basic administrative function or religious role well into the fifth century. The latter function is suggested by Bede's reference to the visit of St Germanus in 429 when he visited the shrine of St Alban. The level of occupation within such towns appears to have been in more or less terminal decline, although it is now suggested that settlement inside the Roman walls at Canterbury was probably continuous from Roman Britain to Anglo-Saxon England. The major issue, of course, is that of making the distinction between continuity of occupation and continuity of authority. On close inspection, the remains of early post-roman settlement within former urban confines are largely indistinguishable from those found in the countryside.

The nature of high-status occupation in fifth-century central and eastern England is very poorly understood. Only the meticulous excavations at Wroxeter by Philip Barker have succeeded in revealing the faint traces of a residence suited in architectural terms to a high-status occupant along with other features including a street. At some point after *c*.375, a date provided by coins, the remains of the Roman Basilica there were finally pulled down and overlain by timber buildings. After an undetermined period of use, these structures were taken down and replaced by two lesser buildings, in turn demolished before an inhumation grave with a radiocarbon date of about 610 was cut.

At the very end of the Roman period dating is a major concern as coins appear not to have been widely used after *c*.400, at which time the mass-production of ceramics also ceased. There seems little reason, however, to ascribe such a late date to urban failure, for archaeological excavations testify to Roman urban decline from at least the third century.

Excavations at Wroxeter, Silchester, Winchester and St Albans all point to complete desertion into the sixth century. At St Albans the excavation of one of the Roman urban properties, *Insula 27*, revealed an extended sequence suggesting occupation well into the fifth century. About 380 a substantial townhouse was built on formerly unoccupied ground. The house comprised 22 rooms in three ranges set around a garden or courtyard; the fourth side of the complex had been destroyed by later activity. After a period of occupation the house was extended by the addition of two rooms, both furnished with mosaic floors. Later, a channelled *hypocaust*, or under-floor heating system, was cut through one of the mosaic floors, but this too happened after a period of occupation sufficient to require the patching of the floor. The stokehole for the hypocaust saw an episode of repair before the entire building was demolished. The site was subsequently used for the erection of a barn, which was itself pulled down prior to the laying of a Roman-style water pipe across the area.

It is commonly the case that the earliest Anglo-Saxon occupation within the confines of Roman towns occurred after a substantial hiatus of inhabitation. A common feature of excavated sequences in towns such as London, Canterbury and Lincoln are thick deposits of mixed dark soil termed 'dark earth'. Some have argued that such deposits were formed by the decay of post-Roman occupation in the form of timber buildings, whilst others suggest ploughing may be responsible for the composition of the soil. Either way a break in settlement is clearly evident.

There is little archaeological evidence from which to reconstruct the lives and social structures of those native Britons who inherited a land characterised by decaying country houses, ruinous towns and collapsed industry from the Roman Empire. Archaeological evidence for post-Roman settlement is best represented in western Britain where the presence of imported ceramics of a known date range has allowed a picture of continued contact between mainland Britain and the Late Roman world to be visualised. There is a range of inscriptions from south-western England that use a devolved form of Latin and these allow for a reconstruction of social organisation in the so-called successor states to the former Roman districts, or *civitates*. Western Britain, however, lies outside the scope of this book and is well covered by the literature.

A different perspective on the nature of settlement and land-use subsequent to the break with Rome is provided by place-names, which suggest a greater degree of overall continuity of populations than any other form of evidence. The scenario of a population slowly reverting to subsistence farming within the context of an unpredictable political scene certainly fits the available evidence.

In the countryside, evidence for the continued occupation of Roman estate centres, or villas, is much harder to assess. The continual build-up of settlement debris found in urban centres at least allows a degree of assessment to be made about the chronology of post-Roman occupation, but rural sites usually lack such deposits. The effects of modern agriculture and the fact that rural settlements are more likely to shift in position than their urban counterparts, often ensures that only the outlines of structures and other features survive. There are all too few rural sites of late Roman date where Early Anglo-Saxon domestic settlement has been identified. Amongst those that have, such as Barton Court Farm, Oxfordshire, the continuity issue is further clouded by the difficulty of ascribing a precise date to the Early Anglo-Saxon phases of settlement.

The archaeological site at Barton Court Farm, excavated by David Miles, revealed a masonry house with eight rooms, which was built within a rectangular enclosure. The building was demolished sometime after *c*.370, although certain ancillary structures survived slightly longer. Subsequently, occupation of an entirely different character was recorded in the form of distinctive 'sunken featured buildings', or SFBs, fence-lines and

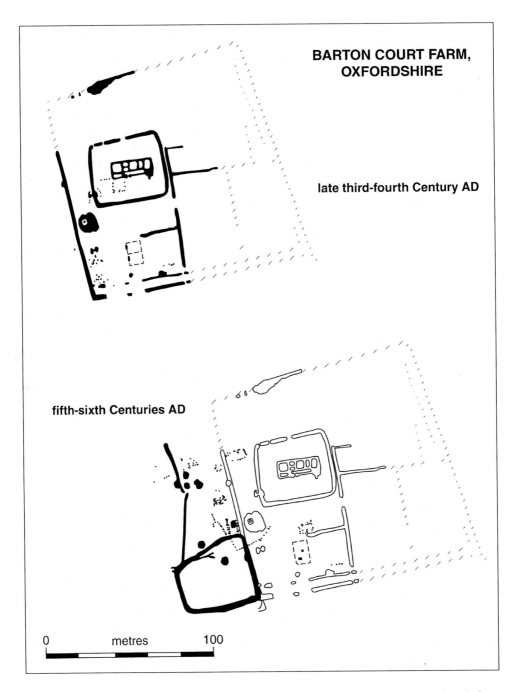

BARTON COURT FARM, OXFORDSHIRE

late third-fourth Century AD

fifth-sixth Centuries AD

0   metres   100

8 *Late Roman and Early Anglo-Saxon settlement at Barton Court Farm, Oxon. Note how little the Roman remains have influenced the layout of the Anglo-Saxon features, suggesting discontinuity of occupation.* Redrawn from Miles 1984

a series of burials. In addition, a ditched enclosure was dug to the south-east of the Roman complex (**8**).

Although it is tempting to read direct continuity into the Barton Court evidence, the archaeological remains do not provide the clarity necessary to support such a view. In fact, it can be argued that the Roman remains were largely ignored with only the northern limit of the Early Anglo-Saxon enclosure respecting the line of an earlier Roman ditch. Such partial survival, or fossilisation, of earlier landscape features is common to all periods of settlement in the British Isles.

SFBs represent a building type unknown in Roman Britain, but are widely attested from contemporary continental sites during the so-called 'migration period'. Such buildings comprise a sub-rectangular pit dug into the ground with a posthole at each end, midway along the end walls (**9**), presumably to take supports for a ridgepole. In a continental context, SFBs are usually interpreted at workshops, whereas British archaeologists for a long period interpreted the English examples as dwellings.

A further type of structure long argued to be of Germanic origin is the timber hall. The majority of late Roman dwellings and estate centres were constructed of stone, and archaeologists had paid too little attention both to ancillary buildings associated with villas and to the nature of lower status rural settlements. Excavations at Dunston's Clump, Nottinghamshire, however, have revealed a Roman farmstead, dating to the third century, characterised by timber buildings formed of upright posts set into individual postholes in the same configuration as halls from the later 'Anglo-Saxon' settlements (**10**). Martin Welch has noted that a British contribution to the architectural repertoire observed on Anglo-Saxon settlement sites is apparent here. If this is so, then it is interesting to note that low-status architecture proved to be the most influential.

As a final point, rural settlements of the later Anglo-Saxon period can be difficult enough to detect in many regions and so the problem of 'missing' fifth-century Britons is probably one of archaeological visibility.

A new cultural identity?

The inability to detect British populations in the form of distinctive burials or settlement remains contrasts strongly with the material culture of fifth- and sixth-century date, which is found earliest within East Anglia, from the beginning of the fifth century. In the main, however, cemeteries containing the graves of individuals buried with artefacts of Germanic design only became widespread during the late fifth and sixth centuries. The broad chronology exhibited by the national distribution of Early Anglo-Saxon cemeteries suggests a gradual movement of migrants from continental Europe, but the new arrivals were derived from a broad geographical area resulting in a rich cultural melting pot from which the English emerged.

In eastern England, archaeological evidence for immediate post-Roman settlement is virtually non-existent. Burials and occupation reveal the first indications of renewed settlement of Germanic character. There is considerable debate about the mechanics of folk movements in the migration period and some scholars have attempted to argue that such a process did not occur at all. For many years archaeologists and historians relied

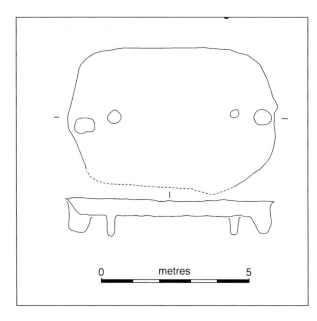

9 *Plan of a typical Sunken Featured Building (SFB) from Mucking, Essex. Note the postholes for roof supports at either end of the structure. Redrawn from Hamerow 1993*

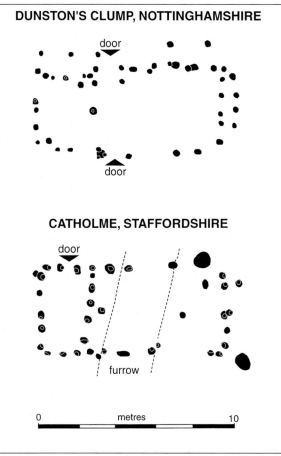

DUNSTON'S CLUMP, NOTTINGHAMSHIRE

door

door

CATHOLME, STAFFORDSHIRE

door

furrow

10 *A Roman timber building of the third century from Dunston's Clump, Nottinghamshire compared to a timber structure from the Middle Anglo-Saxon settlement at Catholme, Staffordshire. Redrawn from Welch 1992*

on a famous passage from Bede's *Ecclesiastical History* as giving a broadly faithful account of the migration process. The passage is from Chapter 15, ostensibly for the year 449, and reads:

> They came from three very powerful tribes of the Germans, namely the Saxons, the Angles and the Jutes. From the stock of the Jutes are the people of Kent and the people of Wight, that is, the race which holds the Isle of Wight, and that which in the province of the West Saxons is to this day called the nation of the Jutes situated opposite that same Isle of Wight. From the Saxons, that is, from the region which now is called that of the Old Saxons, came the East Saxons, the South Saxons, the West Saxons. Further, from the Angles, that is, from the country which is called Angulus, and which from that time until today is said to have remained deserted between the provinces of the Jutes and the Saxons, are sprung the East Angles, the Middle Angles, the Mercians, the whole race of the Northumbrians, that is, those people who dwell north of the river Humber, and the other peoples of the Angles. Their first leaders are said to have been two brothers, Hengest and Horsa, of whom Horsa was afterwards killed by the Britons in battle, and has still in the eastern parts of Kent a monument inscribed with his name. They were the sons of Wihtgils, the son of Witta, the son of Wecta, the son of Woden, from whose stock the royal race of many provinces trace their descent.

When serious academic interest in Early Anglo-Saxon archaeology, principally cemeteries, began in the late nineteenth century, archaeologists set about fitting their data to Bede's narrative account and other sources such as the *Anglo-Saxon Chronicle*. Later on, from the 1920s and 30s, exhaustive studies of particular artefact types, notably pottery and brooches, were mounted. These early studies were largely concerned with the dating and distribution of individual brooch types, which is a worthy exercise in itself but again the historical annals set the archaeologists' agenda. One of the pioneers of such artefact-based studies was E.T. Leeds who excavated and published a series of Early Anglo-Saxon cemeteries, mainly in the Oxford region at sites such as Abingdon and Wheatley. Leeds' artefact typologies have proved to be basically sound, but his interpretations were often strongly historically driven. In one particular article, an attempt was made to link the distribution of an individual type of brooch to the result of an early battle recorded in a much later annal. The most valuable outcome of early research into Anglo-Saxon archaeology was to provide indisputable evidence for a series of major cultural changes beginning in the early decades of the fifth century.

On balance, most archaeologists agree that there was an infusion of Germanic speaking peoples into England beginning in the early fifth century. The emphasis now, however, is very much, as Christopher Scull has put it, upon a sporadic influx of varying intensity and velocity throughout the fifth, sixth and seventh centuries, as opposed to a large-scale mass migration. Research into continued contacts with the Scandinavian world, in combination with England's continuing relationships with the rest of mainland Europe, have suggested

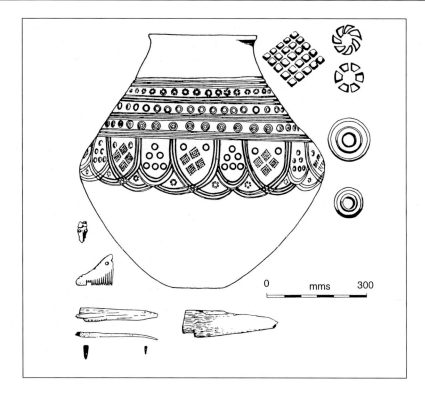

11 *A highly decorated Early Anglo-Saxon cremation urn from Sancton, East Yorkshire. The form and decoration of such containers, as well as the objects often included, was no doubt charged with symbolism relating to the identity of the individual contained within.* Redrawn from Myres and Southern 1973

that the fifth- and sixth- century migrations are best seen as part of a long-term continuum and not as an isolated phenomenon. Although changes in material culture, language, settlement patterns and religion can be accounted for in varying ways, there is little doubt that major social changes occurred from the early part of the fifth century.

Cemeteries containing warrior burials are known from early in the fifth century at sites such as the Roman fort at Richborough in Kent. It is not until slightly later, however, perhaps the 420s onwards, that burial grounds became established in a landscape context and many have argued that the fifth century was a period of loose confederations of warriors with little social structure and with relatively little wealth distinction. Whilst scholars agree in broad terms with this view, a recent study has highlighted the fact that wealth differentiation did exist in the earliest period of Germanic settlement but in a more subtle form.

The Anglo-Saxon burial rite was a varied one. In northern and eastern England large cremation cemeteries are known at sites such as Sancton, East Yorkshire and Spong Hill, Norfolk. Urns, in many cases highly decorated, were used as receptacles for burnt human remains (**11**). The pots were usually placed upright in the ground and in some cases may originally have been sealed with lids. Sometimes objects are found along with cremated bone within urns. Usually, such finds are either the distorted remains of dress fittings and other objects burnt together with the corpse, or miniature objects such as combs and tweezers added to the vessel at the same time as the burnt human remains. At Spong Hill groups of urns were found in addition to individual pots and the large size of the cemetery has suggested to some that the cemetery served a widely dispersed population.

In contrast, the inhumation cemeteries of southern England are generally smaller than their northern counterparts. Although cremation is more widely attested in northern England, there are cemeteries south of the Thames where the practice has been observed, such as Portway, near Andover, and Alton, both in Hampshire. Both the form and decoration of cremation urns from English cemeteries can be directly paralleled by material from contemporary continental sites, particularly in North Germany. Whilst it is possible that a new burial rite bringing with it a new ceramic style was brought about by the exchange of ideas, many still argue that population movement provides the best context for the introduction of cremation.

Julian Richards' work on cremation urns has revealed a link between the dimensions, form and embellishment of individual pots and the cremated individuals that they contain. Quite frequently it is possible to reconstruct a meaningful age and sex profile of a cremated person, and this has allowed Richards to suggest a developed mode of signalling identity using a form of symbolism.

The most widespread form of burial amongst the Early Anglo-Saxons was inhumation; the placing of a body in grave, which might be flat or marked with a post or a mound. The Early Anglo-Saxons were pagans, but all too little is known about the nature of their religion, least of all its practices. The variation of grave construction and grave goods found in individual burials indicates a complex set of social relationships in these early communities with wealth apparently distributed more evenly earlier than later in the period. The inclusion of artefacts within graves suggests that the dead were equipped with the necessary accoutrements for the afterlife. It should be noted, however, that the practice is also likely to be linked to the inheritance customs of individual families or tribes.

Body positioning in Early Anglo-Saxon cemeteries is normally west to east on the back with the hands by the sides or crossed over the pelvis. Exceptions to the norm include prone, or face down burials, decapitations, and double burials and crouched, or flexed burials. The prone burials and decapitations undoubtedly reflect the misdeeds of those so treated and both burial rites are widely attested in the execution cemeteries of the later period. Double burials may well represent the interment of close relatives who died around the same time, perhaps the result of a contagious illness. A more sinister interpretation, however, might be that one of the individuals in each case was put to death, in order to be included in the burial deposit. Crouched burials have been argued to represent those of British stock buried in the cemetery of an Anglo-Saxon community, although the tendency for prone burials to date to the end of the Early Anglo-Saxon period argues against such an 'ethnic' view.

By the sixth century, finds of dress fittings and other material culture from furnished inhumation cemeteries reflects the development of regional identities. In the north and

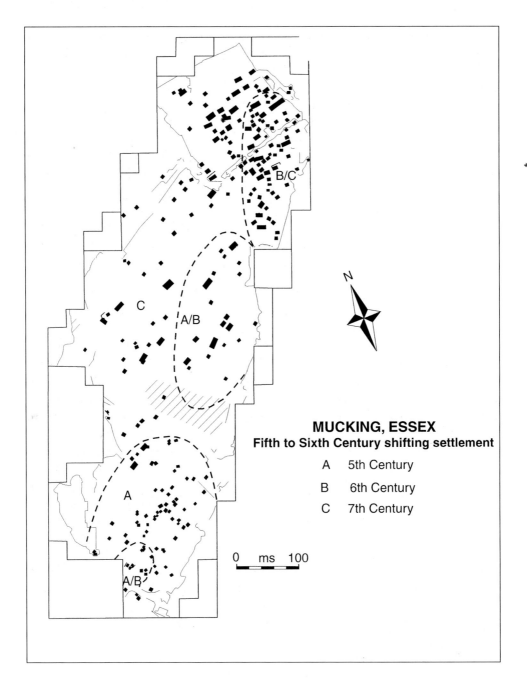

12 *The fifth- to sixth-century settlement at Mucking, Essex. Despite the vast expanse of the settlement remains, only small groups of buildings representing collections of farmsteads were occupied at any one time. Note also how the settlement has shifted across the landscape in an organic fashion.* Redrawn from Hamerow 1993

east cruciform and square-headed brooches and wrist-clasps were distinctive female fashions. From the Thames Valley southward, women's dress styles included saucer brooches, whilst in Kent, metalwork often bears close comparison with Frankish material from across the English Channel.

The earliest excavations on an Early Anglo-settlement took place at Sutton Courtenay, Oxfordshire in the 1920s and 1930s under the direction of E.T. Leeds. Archaeological techniques were still under-developed with regard to such sites and Leeds largely missed certain forms of structural evidence other than SFBs. The post-hole foundations of timber halls, whose floors were at ground level, are partly recognisable from Leeds' plans, but the former presence of more seems likely based on the results of modern settlement excavations. Since Leeds' day there have been a number of excavations notable for their quality, scale, or both. A short discussion of two of these sites, Mucking, Essex and Cowdery's Down, Hampshire will serve to illustrate the character of rural settlements during the fifth to seventh centuries.

Excavations in advance of gravel-quarrying at Mucking uncovered the remains of Anglo-Saxon domestic occupation spanning a period from the fifth to the eighth centuries. In addition to the settlement remains, two cemeteries were located which have led archaeologists to reconsider the hypothesis that Early Anglo-Saxon communities buried their dead on the fringes of their territories or estates. In fact, the number of Early Anglo-Saxon settlements where burial sites lie in close proximity has steadily increased in recent years. One of the most striking features of the Mucking excavations, however, was the sheer size of the area uncovered that measured nearly a kilometre in length and 300 metres in width (**12**). Rather than viewing the remains as a 'site', it is perhaps better to think about Mucking as an excavated landscape. Indeed, most of the settlements and cemeteries of the Early Anglo-Saxon period represent only partially excavated sites and so it is difficult to assess how representative the Mucking remains are of the norm. Overall, 203 SFBs and 53 timber halls were found spread across the site. The earliest occupation dated from the first half of the fifth century but a coin hoard of early eighth-century date and two sherds of Ipswich Ware indicate the longevity of Anglo-Saxon occupation at the site. The lack of stratified deposits including relationships between different phases of buildings led to a phasing based upon a careful analysis of the pottery from individual SFBs, which indicated that the remains represented a shifting hamlet comprising about 10 timber halls and 14 SFBs at any one time. Helena Hamerow has suggested that more than one hamlet may have existed at certain times, although an interim suggestion has put the population of individual phases at about 100 individuals. The material culture of Mucking's inhabitants bears out the range of activities one might expect from a rural community. Finds included a large number of objects used in the weaving process including loom-weights and spindle whorls, whilst imported Frankish pottery and evidence for the production of metal objects testifies to more exotic contacts. On the basis of the settlement density in the Mucking area, Hamerow suggests that the settlement foci moved within a defined territory rather than at random.

At Cowdery's Down in Hampshire excavations by Martin Millett and Simon James uncovered the traces of a pair of modest late sixth- or early seventh-century farmsteads that became superseded by higher status occupation (**13**). Two square enclosures, formed

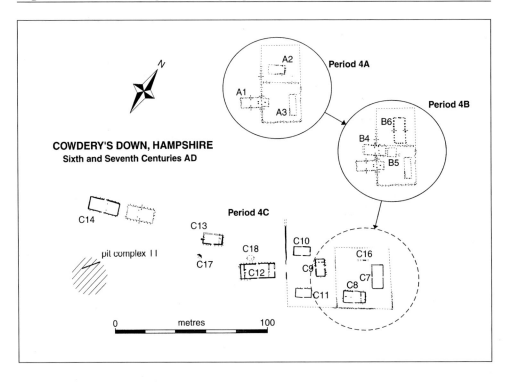

13 *The sixth- to seventh-century settlement at Cowdery's Down, Hampshire. Note how the latest phase of occupation (Period 4C) is characterised by far more elaborate buildings, including two structures positioned end to end (C14 and B/C15).* Redrawn from Millett and James 1983

of lines of individual posts, described areas just over 200m x 200m with timber halls set within each plot. Subsequent activity saw the replacement and addition of timber buildings but the latest Anglo-Saxon phase represents a complete reordering of the site, perhaps in the later half of the seventh century. One of the earlier farm units was retained whilst another was laid out anew. New halls were erected in both units using a newer foundation type; posts set into continuous narrow trenches. Most notably, however, the complex was extended to the west with a range of buildings, impressive in terms of either size or architectural pretension. Careful excavation of the foundation trenches of the later structures has revealed remarkable evidence for the architectural complexity of particular buildings, most impressively in the case of building C12. Only two SFBs were recorded and the contrast between the large number of SFBs at Mucking and the scarcity of examples from Cowdery's Down is most likely related to their underlying geology rather than to functional differences between the sites. Mucking's apparent territorial constraints and the authority manifested in the grander buildings at Cowdery's Down foreshadow the appearance of a much more regulated settlement type characterised by the increasing presence of property boundaries within individual settlements. This process is considered further below, and in Chapter 4.

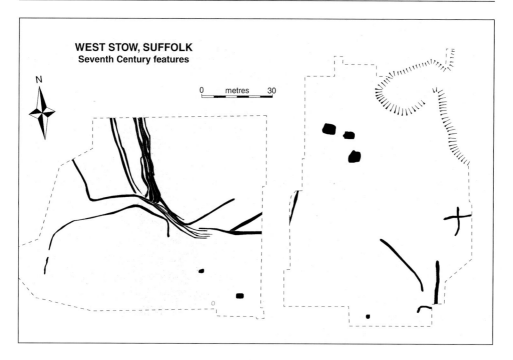

14 *Seventh-century occupation at West Stow, Suffolk. Although the settlement began life in the fifth century, the presence of substantial boundary features belongs only to the latter period.* Redrawn from West 1985

Into the seventh century

The fifth and sixth centuries saw continuous power struggles between groups of warriors attempting to stake and then preserve claims to territory. By the seventh century, documentary sources reveal a country with a very different geographical and political structure to that of later years of the Roman occupation. The landscape had been largely renamed, in English, and dynasties with kingly pretensions ruled kingdoms of varying stability, extent and influence. There is no evidence from the settlements of the fifth and sixth centuries to suggest that social hierarchies existed, but the cemetery evidence does indicate a ranked society reflected in the range of objects of greater or lesser quantity and rarity buried in the cemeteries of the pagan English. It must be said that the cemeteries of the fifth and sixth centuries do not exhibit the extreme polarisation of wealth observed in the burial customs of the seventh century, but they do indicate a scale. Vera Evison has suggested a possible model for pre-Christian social structure based on the relative composition of sets of objects from the 165 graves excavated at the Buckland cemetery near Dover, Kent. Evison identified four types of male graves and five female which were seen to represent rich individuals at the top end of the scale with slaves interred without material possessions at the bottom. Archaeologists have become increasingly critical of such straightforward approaches to interpreting the structure of Early Anglo-Saxon society, but there does seem to be a high level of reliability here given the parallels to be drawn between wealth and status in the documentary record from the earliest Christian centuries.

As noted above, the earliest clear evidence for authority and social ranking is of late sixth- or seventh- century date in settlement terms. During the seventh century however, particularly toward the end, a move towards defining settlement space more rigidly can be observed. The excavated settlement at West Stow in Suffolk, site of the well-known reconstructed Anglo-Saxon village, has revealed clear evidence of this increasing concern for marking the physical extent, probably of newly emerging rights and responsibilities. Although West Stow is known primarily for its Early Anglo-Saxon occupation, including well-preserved SFBs with evidence for raised floors, the latest phase of activity shows evidence for a major reorganisation in the seventh century. A series of boundary ditches was laid out, mainly in the western half of the site but also in the eastern half (**14**). In common with Mucking, relatively soft underlying geology has encouraged the digging of a high proportion of SFBs in relation to timber halls. Nevertheless, the structural remains appear to represent residential halls with ancillary SFBs throughout the life of the settlement, although only a few SFBs represented the structural remains of the latest phase. The addition of the boundary ditches at the site can be seen to describe at least two adjacent enclosures with periodic modifications.

It is only during the seventh century that archaeology begins to be able to bring a sharp focus to the reality of increasing social polarity. A higher degree of ranking and organisation, indicated by the later phases of Early Anglo-Saxon settlements and cemeteries, cannot be doubted to have existed by the early decades of the seventh century. The appearance of settlements containing sometimes large numbers of impressive timber halls, much larger than those at West Stow or Mucking, comes a short time after isolated wealthy burials begin to appear in the late sixth century.

The debate over the origin of kingship is highly complex but can be summarised very briefly. Some historians have stated that the Anglo-Saxons had kings from the earliest post-Roman period, but archaeologists have supplied a cultural narrative that can support the notion that kingship was a late sixth or seventh century creation. The extract from Bede's *Ecclesiastical History* describing the '*adventus Saxonum*', or the arrival of the English, quoted above, contains elements that defy any basis in fact. The reference to three ships, besides being copied from the writings of the sixth century Welsh monk Gildas, has been noted to belong to a broad category or 'origin myths' propagated amongst groups in both England and on the continent. These various 'origin myths' contain other such 'motifs' including the role of pairs of individuals in the earliest histories of individual kingdoms; Hengest and Horsa (Kent), Cerdic and Cynric (Wessex), Stuf and Wihtgar (the Isle of Wight) and Ælle with his two sons (Sussex). The surviving genealogies or lists of descent of the earliest English dynasties eventually dissolve from solid fact into fiction upon close inspection. The use of alliterative formulas, a characteristic of orally transmitted information, can encourage the inclusion of mythical figures, a feature that is most obviously proved by the presence of the pagan god Woden in several lists. Overall, the impression is very much that kingship was created in a short moment in time, which has left us with a clear archaeological dimension to the development of control over extraordinary wealth and power. Indeed, there may well be no precise English comparanda to the structure of the well-known royal burials at Sutton Hoo for precisely the reason that each region reacted to its own unique combination of influences to produce its ideal image of kingship.

The burdens of ruling over territories of continually increasing extent, due to successful military conquest or marriage alliance, fostered the development of embryonic systems of governance. Two discoveries in particular serve to indicate the rapid development, or construction, of a powerful material expression of kingship; the probable royal palace of the Northumbrian kings, including Edwin (616–32), at Yeavering, and the Sutton Hoo cemetery, most likely the burial place of the early East Anglian kings.

Christopher Scull's reinterpretation of the earliest post-Roman phase at the seventh-century royal site at Yeavering provides an example of the fruits of a highly rigorous analysis of excavated evidence. Here it is suggested that the palace phases were preceded by a modest sixth-century settlement of the type considered above, whose dead were buried close-by in a small cemetery centred on a prehistoric monument.

The succeeding activity at the site, however, is characterised by the erection of monumental timber halls and other structures that invite ritual interpretation. Although very few artefacts were found, the frequently striking superimposition of timber halls has allowed a complex stratigraphic sequence to be revealed. The dating of the Yeavering sequence relies heavily on documentary evidence, namely Bede's *Ecclesiastical History*. In Chapter 14 of his history, Bede describes how the recently converted King Edwin of the Northumbrians travelled to the royal residence 'which is known as *ad Gefrin*', with the missionary bishop Paulinus and the Queen of the Northumbrians in the late 620s. The party stayed for 36 days during which Paulinus preached and converted the Northumbrian people who 'flocked to him from all villages and places' for eventual baptism in the nearby river Glen. Bede notes further that the palace at Yeavering was 'deserted in the time of later kings, and another was made instead of it in the place which is called *Maelmin*'. *Maelmin* has been identified as modern Milfield, a short distance to the north east of Yeavering, not only on the basis of the place-name, but also by the recognition of an impressive complex of timber halls revealed by aerial photography.

The Yeavering complex comprised ranges of timber halls built across the top of a notable eminence above the river Glen (**15**). The earliest phase of royal accommodation is believed to predate Paulinus' visit and so a connection with King Edwin's predecessor, King Æthelfrith (592–616) has been proposed and broadly accepted. This phase comprised a substantial timber hall measuring some 25m x 11m with a slightly larger fenced enclosure attached to the east end. The double-fenced Great Enclosure measuring some 150m across lay to the east of the fenced enclosure attached to the timber hall. The absence of a defensive ditch suggests that its primary function was that of a secure stock enclosure. To the west of the hall, lay a cemetery with associated timber buildings, one of them perhaps a pagan temple to judge by the quantity of ox-skulls found within.

The succeeding phase saw the replacement of the hall with two new halls in linear alignment joined to each other by a fenced enclosure. A feature resembling a grandstand was erected during this phase, which probably served as a locus for public assembly and

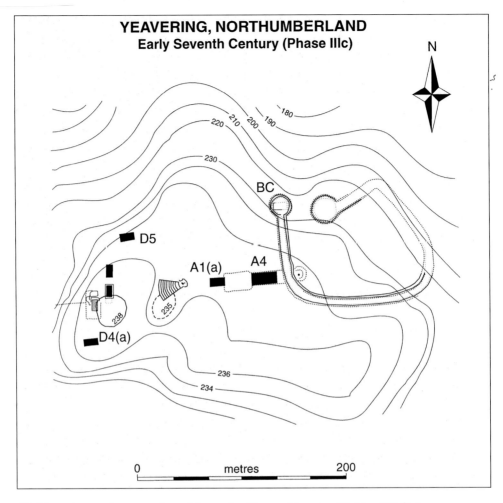

YEAVERING, NORTHUMBERLAND
Early Seventh Century (Phase IIIc)

N

BC

D5

A1(a)   A4

238   235

D4(a)

236

234

0   metres   200

15 *The early seventh-century phase of the royal residence at Yeavering (Bede's ad Gefrin), Northumberland, possibly the palace complex of King Edwin (AD 616–32). Note the linear arrangement of the principal structures including the great hall (A4) and the 'grandstand' for public assembly to the west. The Great Enclosure at the eastern end of the site probably served as a cattle corral.* Redrawn from Hope-Taylor 1977

perhaps for Paulinus' preaching. This phase is attributed to the reign of King Edwin. Successive events at the site included two major fires and the regular replacement of the central halls. After the period ascribed to Edwin, the area of the site contracted with the Great Enclosure, grandstand and western structural and burial complex all out of use by the later seventh century and the reign of King Oswiu (641–70).

The Yeavering site is best interpreted as a place where the king and his retinue stayed periodically, perhaps on a seasonal basis. The various administrative requirements of the newly emergent institution of kingship, such as public assembly and the collection of taxes, could all be served by the existence of royal centres. Besides such practical concerns, the setting and architectural pretensions of the Yeavering complex could not have failed to

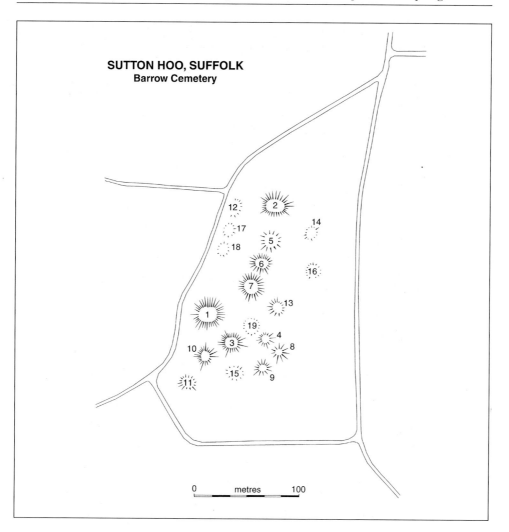

SUTTON HOO, SUFFOLK
Barrow Cemetery

0   metres   100

16 *The high-status barrow cemetery at Sutton Hoo, Suffolk, probably the burial place of the East Anglian royal family, the Wuffingas.* Redrawn from Carver and Hooper 1986

reinforce an impression of wealth, power and stability through the investment of considerable resources in static conspicuous display.

The paucity of material culture from Yeavering is more than compensated for by the material recovered from the royal burial ground at Sutton Hoo in Suffolk. The Sutton Hoo barrow cemetery overlooks the estuary of the river Deben and comprises about 20 mounds built of sand (**16**). Although early antiquarians had disturbed certain of the mounds at the site, excavations in 1939 revealed the splendour of seventh-century kingship in the East Anglian kingdom.

The most impressive funerary deposit was recovered from Mound 1, although Mound 2 also contained a ship-burial, whilst the rite of cremations deposited in bronze bowls has been established in Mounds 4, 5, 6 and 18. A short description of the Mound 1 finds

THE KINGDOMS OF SOUTHERN BRITAIN c. 600 AD

17 *The political geography of seventh-century England showing the seven major kingdoms of Wessex, Mercia, Northumbria, Kent, Sussex, East Anglia and Essex*

will suffice. A fantastic array of grave-finds had been placed within a fine timber ship whose outline survived in remarkable detail as lines of iron clench-nails and stains in the sand. The ship itself was 27m long; in fact it was probably originally longer than the diameter of the mound it lay within. Ostentatious barrow burial is known from the sixth century on the continent, although boat burial of the kind found at Sutton Hoo is an early seventh-century phenomenon at continental sites such as Vendel in Sweden. Indeed, Martin Carver has noted that the Sutton Hoo ship burial could plausibly be amongst the earliest known examples.

The grave finds had been placed within a burial chamber inside the boat and the composition of the assemblage can only represent a reflection of the status of a very powerful warrior, or king. Warrior status is attested by the presence of a fine helmet of Scandinavian type, a coat of mail, a battle-axe and a superb pattern-welded sword with decorative mounts. A tunic in Roman style with gold shoulder-clasps set with garnets, a shield, again of Scandinavian type, and a number of spears make up the rest of the war-gear. The likelihood that the grave is that of a king, however, is strengthened by the presence of objects with highly charged symbolic connotations. A great square-sectioned whetstone tapering toward either end showed no signs of use. Human heads were carved on all four faces of the object close to either end. At the foot of the whetstone, it seems as though a bronze fitting provided support for the object when resting on the knee; it seems that the whetstone was a sceptre. A bronze stag apparently crowned the top of the 'sceptre'. A further object of symbolic significance is the so-called standard; an iron rod with two scrolls at its foot surmounted with an iron cradle and a flat cross-shaped plate at the top. Bede mentions an object called a *'tufa'*, which was carried before King Edwin of Northumbria in his travels and it is plausible that the Sutton Hoo standard represents such an object.

Other objects from the burial included musical instruments, drinking cups, a hoard of coins, a cauldron and chain, and an array of magnificent dress fittings including the famous gold buckle.

Martin Carver's recent excavations at Sutton Hoo have revealed further high-status remains, such as the burial of a warrior with his horse in Mound 17. The discovery of two groups of grisly burials, however, one at the eastern edge of the site and one concentrated upon Mound 5, has brought a new dimension to the realities of early kingship. Although the early law codes from Kent describe a complex system of justice, it is always possible that such codes reflect wishful thinking on the part of the early Kentish kings. The discovery of execution burials at Sutton Hoo though, provides a clear context for the public display of authority by the seventh-century East Anglian aristocracy. Earlier interpretations favoured a sacrificial motivation as part of some pagan ritual, but research by Martin Carver and by the writer has shown that Sutton Hoo conforms to the characteristics exhibited by other Anglo-Saxon execution cemeteries (see Chapter 3, Execution cemeteries). Perhaps Sutton Hoo was much more than simply the burial place of a ruling family, for the cemetery could have performed the role of a tribal centre where assemblies were held, proclamations made and wrongdoers put to death and subsequently displayed.

Summary

Throughout the late fifth and sixth centuries, tribal groups competed with their neighbours for control over land. The sixth century saw the emergence of kingdoms, the nature of which is discussed further below. This process gave rise to a political geography in the early seventh century that comprised only seven major English kingdoms; East Anglia, Essex, Kent, Mercia, Northumbria (comprising the former kingdoms of Bernicia and Deira), Sussex and Wessex (**17**). This period is widely referred to as the 'heptarchy', but the term is rapidly falling out of favour as its frontiers were short lived owing to the emergence of the three most powerful kingdoms; Northumbria, Mercia and Wessex. It is against this political backdrop that the following chapters are set. Our concern is very much with how society was governed and how it lived and worked in a world which, almost in a moment, had become very much more complex.

2 The people: social scales and social relationships

Introduction

The population of England at the time of the Domesday Survey of 1086 has been estimated at some two million people. This short chapter attempts a brief introduction to the various terms used in England before the Norman Conquest to denote rank and status, and to the range of obligations and duties performed among the different strata of society. At the beginning of our period, early charters give an insight into a world where meaningful definitions of superior status were becoming increasingly necessary. The multitude of subservient kings that owed allegiance to their more powerful neighbours required appropriate titles with which to signify their roles in early English politics. Our purpose here, however, is not to deal with the history of effectively political titles, but to examine the nature of social distinction amongst the greater part of the population.

Earlier this century scholars viewed the early English as a largely free society, which operated itself via communal social systems of the type described in the classical writer Tacitus' work *Germania*. Tacitus was writing at the close of the first century AD and his view of continental Germanic society was itself coloured by his own classical world-view. Gradual reassessment of the available evidence has revealed that, at least during the period covered by this book, Anglo-Saxon society was anything but free. It is now widely accepted, for example, that the social and administrative frameworks of Anglo-Norman England owed much more to the efficiency of Late Anglo-Saxon social organisation than to any Norman import. Similarly, the origins of the concept of rural village settlements and the attendant social systems that these imply is now accepted as having originated during the period from the eighth to the tenth century. Finally, about one tenth of the population of eleventh-century England are thought to have inhabited towns. The vast majority of town dwellers were rent-paying tenants, in common with their rural counterparts. Thus, it can be seen that the Anglo-Saxon world was very much an ordered and structured place with clear dividing lines between social classes based upon legal requirements and rights, and the benefits of wealth.

As noted above, Anglo-Saxon society was divided according to a combination of birthright and outright wealth. At the top of the scale came royalty and the higher clergy, but as one moves down the social scale, the mass of the population is divided on the basis of increasing obligations and burdens owed to those above in increasing measure.

Our concern here is with the daily situation, and the discussion below considers the ranks relevant to daily experience, including examples of some of the more regular machinations of later Anglo-Saxon social organisation, such as the freeing of slaves, or manumission. There were essentially few points of departure between the nature of social organisation either side of the Norman conquest of 1066 and it seems that the basic social fabric of later medieval England developed from solid Anglo-Saxon foundations.

The ranks of men and women

The evidence for social ranking and social roles is largely concerned with the situation as it related to men. Anglo-Saxon England, however, is often noted for the fact that women could, and frequently did, hold land and the right to dispose of it. Domesday Book records a Yorkshire-woman Asa, who 'held her land separate and free from the domination and control of Beornwulf her husband, even when they were together, so that he could neither give nor sell nor forfeit it; but after their separation she withdrew with all her land, and possessed it as its lady'. A will dated to between 966 and 975 of a high-ranking woman, Ælfgifu, records 15 estates in her possession, with the majority in Buckinghamshire. Neither were women excluded from playing an active part in legal proceedings; as we shall see below, they could order the freeing of a slave. When one considers the range of documented social roles enacted by women, power was clearly in the hands of the highborn or noble classes. Noble women commonly held high office in the church with the Abbess Hild (Hilda) of Whitby perhaps the most famous of them. Otherwise, the role of women is rarely explicitly described for those of sub-aristocratic status. Specific treatments are prescribed in the fourth law code of King Athelstan (924–939) for female slaves who commit offences, in this case it is burning. Unfortunately, however, there is all too little material from which to reconstruct the roles and responsibilities of the wives and daughters of the better-recorded *thegns* and *ceorls*.

A freeman's life had a monetary value placed upon it called *wergeld*, which literally means 'man's price' or 'man's payment'. The value of the *wergeld* increased in relation to the status of the person, with high-value *wergelds* interpreted as a means of controlling powerful but unruly individuals. There was a complicated list of payments to which reference could be sought for all types of bodily injury from the earliest law code of Æthelberht of Kent in the early seventh century. In late ninth-century Wessex, Alfred acknowledged Æthelberht's laws in his own extensive law code. This situation suggests that Æthelberht's list was either widely adopted or had similar counterparts in other kingdoms, although, apart from Alfred's laws, there is no English tariff of comparable detail.

The majority of offences were settled by the payment of compensation to the injured party, or of fines, usually to the king, but sometimes shared with the church. A fine payable to the king or other public body was usually termed '*wite*', whereas '*bot*' was applied to any kind of compensation. One purpose of the system of fines was to limit blood feud, a primitive and potentially uncontrollable method of exacting justice that did little to enhance kingly pretensions with regard to their public authority. By introducing formal procedure into the settlement of disputes, a mechanism existed by which family pride was allowed proper expression but in a controlled manner avoiding bloodshed.

The most significant division of social class in Anglo-Saxon England was between the free and the unfree. Accordingly, the punishment that an individual was to receive, if found guilty of an offence, was determined by social status. A person's rank affected the level of compensation that was to be received or paid for a given offence and, although certain terms used to denote rank did not remain static over time, the same basic principles appear not to have changed.

The highest rank was that of the king whose *wergeld* was of such a value as to act as safeguard to his life in the face of possible assassination. In late seventh-century Wessex, in the time of King Ine, a 30-fold compensation is known to have been enforced, whilst in Mercia, after the eighth century, the king's *wergeld* was 12 times that of a noble. Similarly large amounts were set in Northumbria.

The next social positions were the *ealdorman*, an important councillor, royal deputy and regional official, and the *gesith*, a well-born man with military obligations. In Northumbria the term *gerefa* seems to have been applied to persons with a similar status to the *ealdorman*. The attribution of *gesithcund* (*gesith*-born) status did not, however, imply a specific office of state. This term, which was not exclusive to men, was current during the reign of Ine but it had lost its political significance by the time of Alfred. A *gesithcund* man had a *wergeld* of 1200 shillings in Wessex, which was equivalent to 300 gold shillings in Kent. Up to the time of Alfred the term *eorl* was used to signify superior rank and was the sole indicator of a superior social class to appear in the earliest Kentish laws. Some idea of the material possessions of a high-status male can be gained by reference to the war-gear, or *heriot*, that he should ideally possess. *Heriot* meant rather more than simply the physical equipment of a warrior, for it represented the gift of weaponry made by a lord to one entering his retinue, and which was returnable upon the death of a man. The *heriot* of one tenth-century ealdorman is listed as 'four armlets of 300 mancuses of gold, and four swords and eight horses, four with trappings and four without, and four helmets and four coats-of-mail and eight spears and eight shields.' If a warrior fell in battle, however, the requirement to return the war-gear or equivalent was waived.

During the reign of Alfred, the term *thegn* came into common usage. In origin, a *thegn* was a servant of the king with a *wergeld* of 1200 shillings and, until the tenth century, he was normally a household officer of a great man. The kings' *thegns* held a more elevated social position, with a *heriot* only just below half of that of the *ealdorman*, and they served the monarch more directly than their lowlier counterparts. After this time the term could apply to a wide variety of personal situations from those with great privileges down to simple retainers. The most powerful *thegns* held vast tracts of land. Wulfric Spott, a wealthy *thegn* of the northern Danelaw, and founder of the monastery at Burton-on-Trent in 1004, owned 72 estates spread largely throughout Staffordshire and Derbyshire, but with others in Warwickshire, Shropshire, Leicestershire, Yorkshire, Gloucestershire, Worcestershire and Lincolnshire. He held further lands of unknown extent on the Wirral Peninsula and in South Lancashire. The other end of the scale represented a wholly different scenario. An estate at Salden in Buckinghamshire, of a little over three hides in extent, represents a very small holding by comparison to the Late Anglo-Saxon norm of five hides or multiples of five. The Salden estate, however, despite its small size, was divided between four individuals of *thegnly* rank, who were

59

themselves men of other lords. The contrast between the social position of Wulfric Spot and the Salden *thegns* is considerable.

Importantly, by the eleventh century at least, *thegnly* rank could be either inherited or acquired by the accumulation of certain attributes described in a compilation known as *Geþyncðo*, or 'concerning *wergilds* and dignities', dated to the early eleventh century. The clause from *Geþyncðo* reads 'And if a ceorl prospered, that he possessed fully five hides of land of his own, a bell and a burh-gate, a seat and special office in the kings hall, then was he henceforth entitled to the rights of a thegn'. A twelfth-century document from Rochester preserves a slightly different version, adding a 'church and kitchen' and a 'bell-house' to the list. Clearly there are archaeological implications to this description of *thegnly* accommodation and these are explored below in Chapter 4. A further clause from *Geþyncðo* relates that 'if a trader prospered, that he crossed thrice the open sea at his own expense, he was then afterwards entitled to the rights of a thegn'. Evidently a prosperous merchant could cross social divides along with his rural counterparts. One of the most crucial sources for social organisation towards the end of our period is a treatise on estate management known as the *Rectitudines Singularum Personarum*. The document notes a range of *thegnly* responsibilities, which are largely military but which also include mending the 'deer-fence' at the king's residence and attendance on his superior. The military role of the *thegn* is considered further in Chapter 3 under the topic of civil defence.

The clergy had a special scale of *wergeld* but should a man in orders be of noble birth then the *wergeld* pertaining to the latter status was preferred.

The ordinary freeman was a *ceorl* with a *wergeld* of 200 shillings. Besides connotations of social rank, the term *ceorl* was applied across the social scale with the additional meaning of 'husband'. Over time the level of involvement of the *ceorl* in matters of defence and in the courts declined although obligations to public duties in the army and the courts continued to play a central role in both urban and rural communities. In addition, *ceorls* were required to contribute to the *feorm*, or food rent, necessary to support the king and his retinue for one night. This burden is attested from the middle Anglo-Saxon period and survived in a vestigial form in the south west until after the Norman conquest. The *Rectitudines Singularum Personarum* describes several variations within the sub-*thegnly* class that show just how variable the role of the Anglo-Saxon *ceorl* could potentially be. Below the status of a *thegn* comes a social class termed *geneats* who Sir Frank Stenton has described as forming a peasant aristocracy. Amongst general upkeep of the estate, a *geneat* performed a range of tasks including carrying messages 'far and near', conducting strangers or visitors to the estate centre, cartage of his lords provisions and produce and standing guard over horses. The *geneat's* role as one that 'attends' and 'entertains' his lord suggests a social rank somewhat akin to a modern foreman or farm manager. Eric John has noted that the *ceorl* Dunnere, who fought with Earl Byrhtnoth at the Battle of Maldon in Essex in 991, was part of the Earl's retinue; a fitting role perhaps for one of *geneat* rank. Both *thegn* and *geneat* were required to pay alms, but church dues extended down to the next social grouping as described in the *Rectitudines*, the *cotsetla* or *cottar*. The *cottar* paid no rent for his ground, but he was expected to work at least five acres of land with at least one day per week devoted to serving his lord, with up to three days per week required at harvest time. The maintenance of the king's deer-fence was part of the *cottar's* responsibility along with military service.

A larger mass of the working population belonged to a social class known as the *geburas*. The *gebur* had heavier burdens with regard to services rendered on the estate and included working on the lord's estate for two days per week all year round, with heavier burdens at harvest and in early spring. It is clear from the *Rectitudines* that the *gebur* received from his lord two oxen, one cow, six sheep and seven acres sown and the necessary 'tools for his work and utensils for his house'. Rents, however, were paid in cash and in kind and were collected at Michelmas (10 pence), Martinmas (23 sesters of barley, and two hens) and Easter (one lamb or two pence). Further burdens for tenants such as the *gebur* included giving six loaves of bread to the swineherd when his herd is driven to pasture and supporting one of the lord's hounds jointly with another tenant. The *gebur* may have qualified as a freeman in legal terms but his existence and that of his family would have been greatly influenced by lordly authority.

It is all too infrequently noted that the Christian Anglo-Saxons were a slave-owning society, although it is difficult to asses the level of slavery at any given time. There was in Kent, in the time of Æthelberht at least, a class of half-free men called *litus*, a term which had become extinct before the time of Alfred, although slaves were in general graded according to their abilities and to whom they belonged. Slaves, or *thralls* as they were termed, could be owned not only by royalty and the higher-ranking individuals, but also by *ceorls*. Slavery of an individual might result from birth into that particular social class, although penal slaves and prisoners of war are likely to have formed a significant component of what Eric John has argued to have been the most heavily populous of the social classes.

In the event of a lawsuit, concern was concentrated on compensation of the slave's owner as opposed to any measure designed to safeguard the slave himself or herself. Indeed, a master without redress to the formal courts could subject a slave to corporal or even capital punishment. The late seventh-century laws of king Wihtred of Kent, however, give a number of prescriptions in favour of slaves, such as the clause which describes the outcome 'if a servant, by his lord's command, do[es] servile work between sunset on Saturday evening and sunset on Sunday evening, his lord is to pay 80 shillings'. In common with the *ceorls*, social mobility was possible, if relatively uncommon. This process is illuminated by the small number of surviving manumissions performed during the reigns of the tenth-century kings. Women slaves could be granted free status, on occasion by another woman. A manumission performed by Æthelflæd, wife of a powerful Wessex Ealdorman, at the turn of the tenth and eleventh centuries, which itself gives some indication of the level of responsibilities that could fall within the remit of a high-ranking woman, reads:

> This is the name of the woman, Ælfgyth, whom Æthelflæd freed for her soul and for the soul of her lord, Ealdorman Æthelweard, on the bell of St Petroc in the residence which is called Liskeard, in the presence of these witnesses looking on: Athelstan the priest, Wine the priest, Dunstan the priest, Goda the thegn, Ælfweard Scirlocc, Æthelwine Muf, Ealdred his brother, Eadsige the writer. And these are the witnesses from the clerics of St Petroc's: Prudens the priest, Boia the deacon, Wulfsige the deacon,

Brihtsige the cleric, in order that freedom... And afterwards Ealdorman Æthelweard came to the minster of St Petroc and freed her for his soul on the altar of St Petroc in the presence of these witnessess looking on: Bishop Burhwold, Abbot Germanus, Tittherd the priest, Wulfsige the deacon, Wurgent, son of Samuel, Ylcaerthon the reeve, Tethion the 'consul'... the son of Mor. And he affirmed that whosoever shall observe this liberty shall be blessed, and whosoever shall infringe it shall be cursed by the Lord God of heaven and by his angels. Amen.

The lot of the slave was clearly a poor one, but their role in underpinning the agricultural economy of individual estates was probably considerable. Although slaves in Anglo-Saxon England were probably largely free from physical abuse or bodily constraint, the mental condition of the rural *thrall* is appropriately summed-up in a late tenth- or early eleventh-century source, a Latin schoolbook known as the *Colloquy* of Abbott Ælfric. The reply of a ploughman to a questioner who asks him about his work runs: 'It is a great toil... because I am not free'.

Although the value of written sources such as the *Rectitudines Singularum Personarum* is immense, it should always be borne in mind that considerable regional and even local variation existed with regard to custom and practice. Indeed, a reservation noted in the *Rectitudines* itself serves to illustrate the issue from a contemporary perspective:

'This estate law exists on certain estates; at some places, as I have said, it is heavier, at some places also lighter; for all estate customs are not alike. On some estates a tenant must pay tax in honey, on some tax in food, on some tax in ale. He who looks after the administration is to take care that he always knows what is the ancient arrangement on the estate, and what is the custom of the people'.

A further source of evidence for those interested in Anglo-Saxon social structure are place-names that preserve, usually in an altered form, a pre-conquest term of reference to a social class or rank. At the upper end of the scale are names containing 'king' (Old English *cyning*). Examples include Kingston (the king's farm) and Kingsland (the king's land) type names. A connection with royalty is indicated too by names containing Old English *fengel*, or *æðeling*, both meaning 'prince'. Examples include Finglesham, or 'the prince's homestead', in Kent, and 'prince's farmsteads' at Athelington, Suffolk, and Allington, recorded in Dorset, Lincolnshire and Wiltshire. Athelney in Somerset, meaning 'prince's Island', is mentioned in the *Anglo-Saxon Chronicle* under the year 878, when King Alfred and his party received 30 leading men on behalf of the recently defeated Danish army, for baptism at Aller close to Athelney. The powerful regional officials, or *ealdormen*, of the Late Anglo-Saxon period have left their mark in the modern place-name record in Aldermaston, Berkshire and in the Aldermanbury names preserved in London and Bedford. The shire-reeve, or sheriff, a man responsible for a shire in the Late Anglo-Saxon period and answerable to a regional *ealdorman*, has left his mark as a place-name in Shrewton, Wiltshire, Shroton, Dorset and Shurton, Somerset. The 'ton' element in these latter names literally means farmstead, giving the grand title 'farm of the shire-reeve' to the official's residence.

The *thegnly* classes are referred to directly in Thenford, Northamptonshire and indirectly by reference to the fortified structure, or *burh-geat*, referred to in the *Geþyncðo* as a requirement of *thegnly* status. Examples of Burgate as a modern place-name are not overly frequent but examples are known across southern and eastern England from Hampshire, Suffolk, Surrey and Sussex. A further possibility is Yatesbury, Wiltshire, which might simply represent a reordering of '*burh-geat*'.

Of all the social classes of Anglo-Saxon England, *ceorls* have left the most substantial mark in the modern landscape. 'Charlton', meaning '*ceorl's* farm', occurs widely as a place-name in central and south-western England. Other variations with regard to spellings include Charleton, Devon, Charlston, Sussex and Chorlton, Lancashire. The homesteads of *ceorls* are recorded in names such as Charlacott, Devon and Charlecote, Wiltshire, but ceorl's are never found in compound with *ham*, or 'homestead' type names. This scenario has suggested to some that the *ceorl's* tun was a distinct type of farming settlement set apart from, but in close proximity to, an important local centre of administration. The Old English word for 'a payer of tax, rent or tribute', *gafolmann*, is attested in Galhamton and Galmington, Somerset, whilst examples of Galton are found in both Devon and Dorset. These settlements were undoubtedly coterminous with the ceorl's tun's; other place-names incorporating *gafol* largely relate either to rented land, as in Gavelacre, Hampshire, or to the existence of a toll-bridge or ford.

Thralls, or slaves, are very rarely recorded in modern place-names but examples are known such as Threlkeld, Cumbria, meaning '*thrall's* spring'.

With an impression of how Anglo-Saxon society was organised in terms of social ranking, it is appropriate now to consider the territorial and administrative frameworks within which the different groups described above lived and worked together.

3 The landscape: territorial arrangements and governance of the realm

Introduction

It can be said with great confidence that the basic frame of much of the modern landscape was the product of Anglo-Saxon local and regional planning. Organised social systems might be imposed from above or instigated by common consent, but both have the potential to be revealed by archaeological fieldwork and documentary research. This chapter looks at the archaeological and historical evidence for governance and civil works in Anglo-Saxon England, including public assembly, civil defence and judicial execution. In the main, archaeologists have only recently begun to explore aspects of 'administrative archaeology' beyond the study of King Alfred and his successors' fortified towns of the late ninth and early tenth centuries.

Early kingdoms and the origins of the shires

The system of shires, as it remained up until the great 1974 boundary revision, was essentially that which existed by the middle of the eleventh century (**18**). The word 'shire' is derived from Old English *scir*, meaning simply 'share'.

The shires had varied origins. Both Bede and early charters record the existence of distinct administrative units called *regiones*. These districts seem to have served as sub-divisions of sixth- to eighth-century kingdoms, which probably relate to conquered territories or politically dominated sub-kingdoms. The evidence of place-names is of the greatest importance for the reconstruction of these early territories in any detail.

Certain counties, such as Suffolk and Norfolk, and distinct territorial units such as the Isle of Ely described as a *regio* by Bede, appear to retain the integrity of late sixth- and seventh-century territories within the seventh-century kingdom of East Anglia. Certainly, the presence of bishops in both Norfolk and Suffolk during the seventh century gives an impression of the former importance of these units. Such large units were formed of an amalgam of embryonic 'micro-kingdoms', the outcome of the struggle for territory that accompanied the development of kingship from the late fifth to the eighth centuries. Steven Bassett has compared the struggle for control of territory in seventh-century

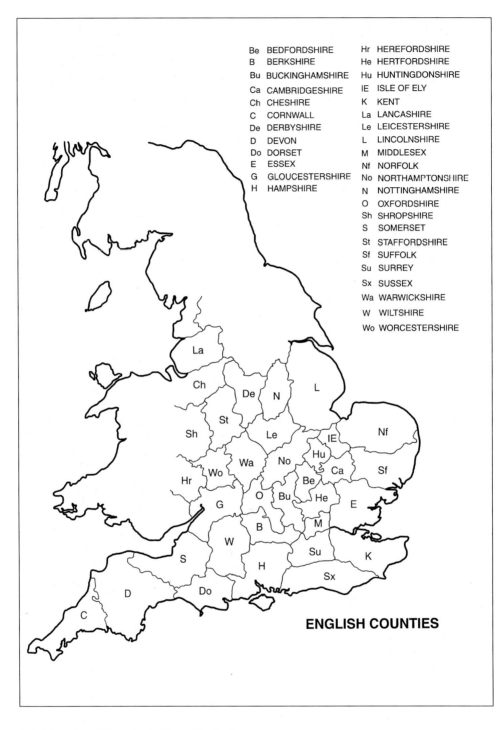

Be	BEDFORDSHIRE	Hr	HEREFORDSHIRE
B	BERKSHIRE	He	HERTFORDSHIRE
Bu	BUCKINGHAMSHIRE	Hu	HUNTINGDONSHIRE
Ca	CAMBRIDGESHIRE	IE	ISLE OF ELY
Ch	CHESHIRE	K	KENT
C	CORNWALL	La	LANCASHIRE
De	DERBYSHIRE	Le	LEICESTERSHIRE
D	DEVON	L	LINCOLNSHIRE
Do	DORSET	M	MIDDLESEX
E	ESSEX	Nf	NORFOLK
G	GLOUCESTERSHIRE	No	NORTHAMPTONSHIRE
H	HAMPSHIRE	N	NOTTINGHAMSHIRE
		O	OXFORDSHIRE
		Sh	SHROPSHIRE
		S	SOMERSET
		St	STAFFORDSHIRE
		Sf	SUFFOLK
		Su	SURREY
		Sx	SUSSEX
		Wa	WARWICKSHIRE
		W	WILTSHIRE
		Wo	WORCESTERSHIRE

ENGLISH COUNTIES

18 *The shires of Late Anglo-Saxon England*

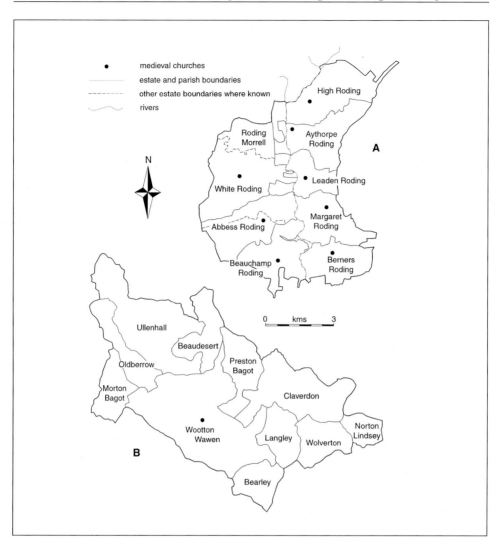

19 *Early micro-kingdoms. **A** the Roding parishes in Essex and **B** the regio of the Stoppingas reflected by the extent of the minster parochiae of Wotton Wawen, Warwickshire.* Redrawn from Bassett 1989

England to a football championship knockout competition, with smaller kingdoms surviving until they are absorbed by the outward expansion of the frontiers of more powerful neighbours. Recent studies of early micro-kingdoms in Essex and Warwickshire have revealed the nature and extent of certain of these early territories (**19**) and Bassett suggests that the documented administrative districts of the tenth century and later, the hundreds, may often preserve their morphology.

In Essex, a group of eight ecclesiastical parishes are named Roding in combination with a variety of post-conquest additions, such as Berners, Morrell and Beauchamp. Domesday

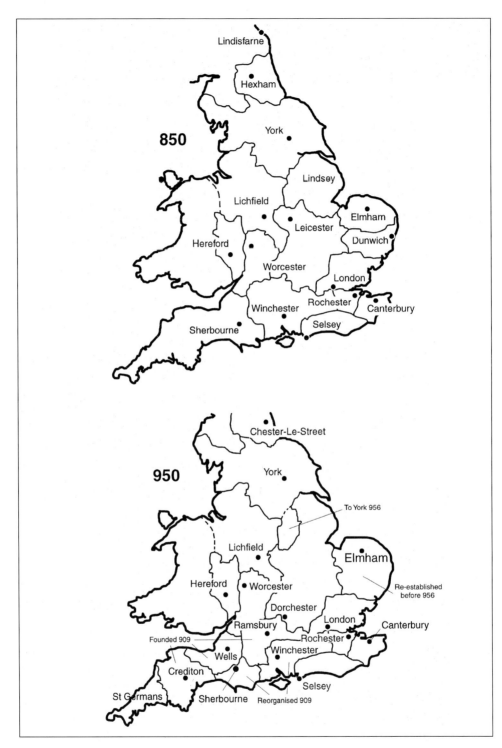

20 *Diocesan boundaries before and after the creation of the Danelaw in AD878*

Book, however, lists 16 estates all referred to simply as *Rodinges* or *Roinges*. In Old English, Roding means 'the people of Hrotha' and by drawing a line around the extent of the Roding parishes a plausible map of an early territory can be arrived at. Minor boundary changes are likely to have occurred as part of an organic process associated with the exchange of small parcels of land by will or sale, although the extent of the Rodings agrees well with the kind of area one might expect an organised grouping to occupy. The area occupies part of the River Roding valley, with roughly equal lands on either side of the river and provides good access to a wide range of resources for its inhabitants.

A reconstruction by Steven Bassett of the *regio* of a Warwickshire group called the *Stoppingas* has been made possible by a careful consideration of a range of sources. A charter of King Æthelbald of Mercia (716–57) of early eighth-century date mentions both the *regione,* and the *Stoppingas* themselves. The charter itself deals with a grant of 20 hides to a monastery at Wootton Wawen. The geographical extent of the *regio*, however, can be established with knowledge of the extent of the parish, or *parochia*, served by the minster church. The resultant area is both cohesive in its composition and comparable in size to the Roding territory described above.

The evidence of diocesan boundaries and minster church parishes, or *parochiae* provides a profitable approach to the reconstruction of early territories, although the disruption caused to the diocesan geography of England by the Viking incursions should always be borne in mind (**20**). Each diocese was centred on an important church, although individual minster churches, each with a discreet *parochia*, dealt with the everyday business of Christianity within each diocese. It appears as though certain diocesan divisions, prior to the ninth-century disruption brought by the Vikings, were laid out with respect to pre-existing kingdoms. Such an interpretation is certainly the most logical. Before the development of parishes from the tenth century, the Middle Anglo-Saxon landscape was characterised by minster, or mother, churches that served extensive *parochiae*. Although there was an increase in the number of minsters during the Middle Anglo-Saxon period, seventh-century foundations on former royal lands are known from documentary sources. Again, the assumption is that seventh-century *parochiae* are likely to be coterminous with pre-existing territorial arrangements. This scenario certainly agrees with the pattern of the conversion of the English to Christianity, which, first and foremost, was fertilised amongst the newly emerged royal dynasties.

Historical research has met with some success with regard to producing a picture of administrative arrangements in the early English Kingdoms in combination with the information provided by a remarkable, probably late seventh-century taxation assessment known as the Tribal Hidage (**21**). The Tribal Hidage comprises a list of the landholdings of 35 named tribes, most of whom can be located by surviving place-names. The list survives in an eleventh-century document, although the political scene that it describes is much earlier, perhaps *c.*680. Some prefer to see the list as a Mercian tribute list of late seventh- to mid-eighth-century date, whilst a ninth- or tenth-century West Saxon origin is not out of the question given the extraordinary hidage assessment for that kingdom (100,000 hides). A further view is that the compilation was assembled in the tenth century, incorporating certain earlier material. The list includes all of the major seventh-century kingdoms, with the exception of Northumbria, and at least the basis for the

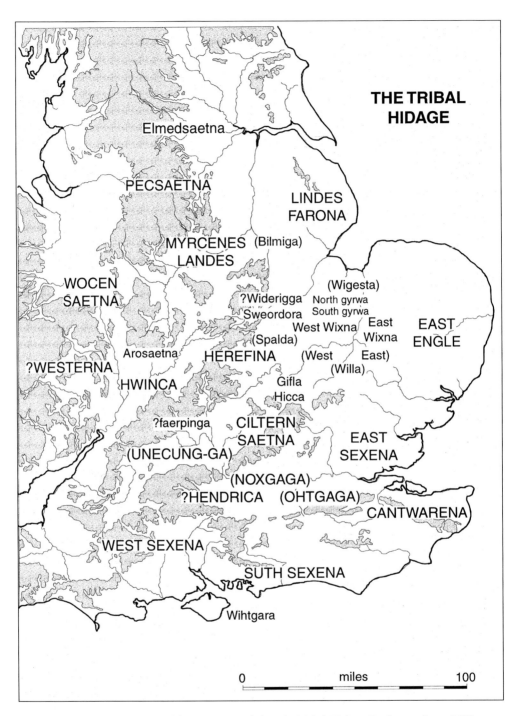

21 *The geographical locations of the groups recorded in the Tribal Hidage.* Redrawn from Hill 1981

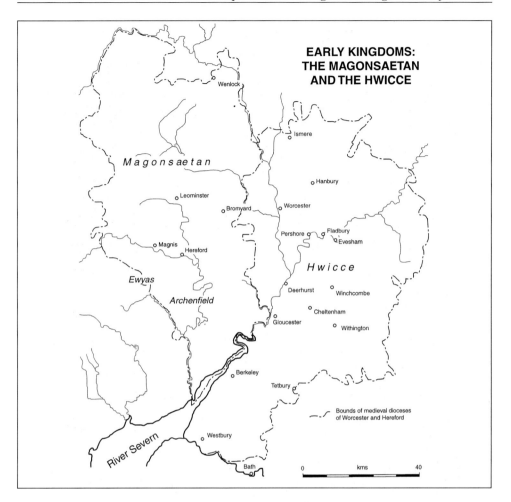

22 *The kingdoms of the Hwicce and the Magonsæte fossilised by the boundaries of the diocese of Worcester and Hereford.* Redrawn from Hill 1981

document is broadly accepted as late seventh century in date. Further early or at least pre-conquest written sources refer to lands not mentioned in the Tribal Hidage, which probably means that the list is incomplete. Alternatively, rapid political developments of the seventh century could account for the short-lived existence of a micro-kingdom. The Tribal Hidage should therefore be seen as a snapshot of early England rather than representing any fixed political frontiers of particular longevity.

The various lands are assessed in terms of units called 'hides'. Bede tells us that the hide was *terra unius familiae*, or 'land sufficient to support one family', and provides us with some territorial assessments to compare with the Tribal Hidage. The unit remained in use throughout the Anglo-Saxon period as the standard measure for land assessment. It appears that the hide itself was determined by aspects of productivity rather than a specified area, although it is generally held that in Wessex the hide roughly equated to 120

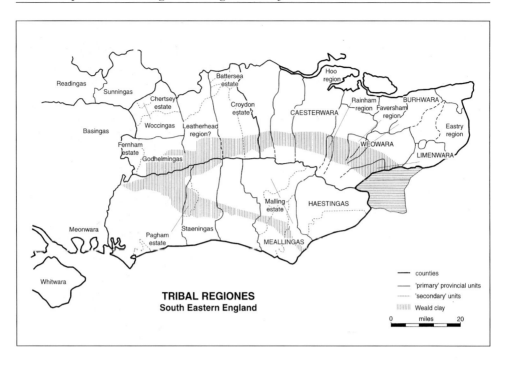

23 *Tribal regiones in south-eastern England.* Redrawn from Blair 1989

acres (49 ha) of land. By the later Anglo-Saxon period issues such as social mobility and military service were determined using the hide as the basic tenurial unit, whereas land charters of both Middle and Late Anglo-Saxon date most commonly record multiples of five- or ten-hide units of land.

The Tribal Hidage records a wide range of territories in terms of differences in hidage assessments. Smaller groups occur mainly in the East Midlands and the East Anglian Fenland. The *Cilternsaete* (the Chilterns area) assessed at 4000 hides, down to the *Gifla* (based in the Ivel valley in Bedfordshire) with as little as 300 hides give some impression of the range. A number of tribes in the West Midlands had assessments of 7000 hides, including the *Hwinca*, probably the *Hwicce* — a tribe in the south-west Midlands, the *Westerna* — probably the *Magonsaete*, based around Roman *Magnis* (now Kenchester) Herefordshire and the *Wocensaete*, whose name survives in the Wrekin, Shropshire. The territories of the *Hwicce* and the *Magonsæte* can be realised on a map by plotting the boundaries of the diocese of Worcester and Hereford that respectively served these early kingdoms (**22**). When plotted onto a map, the charters issued by the kings of the *Hwicce* exhibit a close correlation with the limits of the diocese of Worcester, thus demonstrating the validity of such an approach elsewhere.

The south western shires, including Somerset, Dorset, Wiltshire and Hampshire appear to be of late seventh- or eighth-century origin. The earliest surviving West Saxon laws of King Ine (688–726) record that a man should pay a fine of 60 shillings to his lord if he 'steals into another shire'. Although the term may not have had quite the same precise territorial connotations as in later times, some element of jurisdiction is implied.

From the eighth century the evidence for shires in Wessex becomes explicit. *The Anglo-Saxon Chronicle* mentions *Hamtunscir* under the year 750, which relates the territory to the archaeologically attested trading settlement of Hamwic. This aspect ties in well with the names of other Wessex shires, which are named after their principal settlements; Wiltshire is named from Wilton and Somerset from Somerton. Devon, however, derives its name from the sub-Roman kingdom of *Dumnonia* and Barbara Yorke has compared this aspect to Sussex and Essex as examples of former kingdoms fossilised as West Saxon shires.

By the tenth century Wessex had absorbed the south eastern counties, but these too have retained in varying degrees aspects of their integrity as distinct territories (**23**). Kent is a further unit that survived the transition from kingdom to shire, but, in common with Sussex, there was a territorial division below that of the shire but above that of the hundred. Kent was divided into six districts known as Lathes, whereas the equivalent units in Sussex are known as Rapes. There are strong indications that these particular subdivisions pre-date the shires and represent early *regiones* of the type familiar to Bede, although the Sussex rapes as viewed at the time of Domesday Book are Norman lordships, seemingly created as a defensive measure in relation to the coastline.

Berkshire has different origins again, and appears to represent a slightly later formation than the other Wessex shires. Margaret Gelling has noted the artificial appearance of the boundary between Berkshire and Hampshire. Indeed, the boundary is remarkably straight and has been observed to cut through both ecclesiastical and secular land units. This disregard for existing divisions of the landscape has lead historians to suggest that the formation of Berkshire occurred during the series of wars between the West Saxons and the Mercians during the course of the eighth century and into the early ninth century. It is known that the northern part of Somerset, Wiltshire and probably all of Berkshire, was part of the Mercian kingdom during the second half of the eighth century. Western Berkshire is characterised by chalk downland and Jeremy Haslam and others have suggested early origins for what were later known as the hundreds of Lambourne and Kintbury that adjoin the eastern boundary of Wiltshire. Eastern Berkshire is apparently composed of two earlier territories, or *regiones*; the *regio* of the *Readingas* (people of the Reading area) and the *regio* of the *Sunningas* (people of the Sonning area). The name of the shire itself, however, is derived from *Barroc*, a British name, probably for the west Berkshire Downs. After their early origins, the social and political developments of the eighth century and later ensured that the Wessex shires developed into clearly defined administrative territories with fixed boundaries.

We have mentioned Norfolk and Suffolk above, but the other eastern counties, such as Essex, Cambridgeshire and Huntingdonshire have origins either as distinct territories or kingdoms prior to their later role as administrative subdivisions of larger kingdoms. The northern counties are difficult to reconstruct before the eleventh century owing to effects of Danish control of Northern and Eastern England in the late ninth and early tenth centuries. In the north east, the *Anglo-Saxon Chronicle* entry for 876 directly describes the fate of the estate and administrative geography prior to that date as 'that year Healfdene shared out the land of the Northumbrians, and they [the Vikings] proceeded to plough

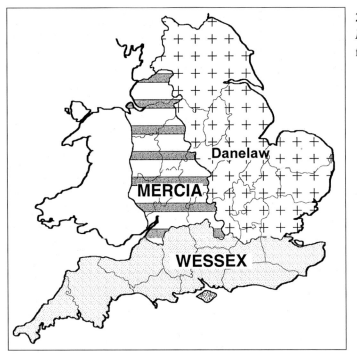

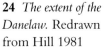

24 *The extent of the Danelaw.* Redrawn from Hill 1981

and support themselves'. Two years later, King Alfred's victory over the Danish King Guthrum resulted in the division of England into the West Saxon Kingdom and the Danelaw, literally 'the territory under Danish law' (**24**). We are fortunate that a later copy of a treaty of the 880s, describing the course of the Danelaw boundary, survives. The document is known as the Treaty of Alfred and Guthrum and after a short introduction the opening paragraph reads:

> 'First as to the boundaries between us. [They shall run] up the Thames, and then up the Lea, and along the Lea to its source, then in a straight line to Bedford, and then up the Ouse to Watling Street.'

In general terms, there is agreement among scholars that the administrative geography of the West Saxon kingdom preserves a greater archaic element than that found in the Danelaw areas. This scenario appears likely based upon the extraordinary contrast that can be observed between the frequently variable size and irregular boundaries of shire and hundredal units in Wessex and the more regular divisions observed in the equivalent boundaries of the Danelaw. From this point, however, there are some who suggest that the differences are due to the Anglo-Saxons imposing a model shiring system on re-conquered Danelaw regions, whereas others prefer to see the system as a Viking 'import'. On balance, the evidence supports the argument for an imposed West Saxon model administrative geography, although some allowance should be made for earlier territorial patterns, such as those imposed or utilised by Danish settlers and landlords, to have been at least partly preserved.

The reconquest of the Danelaw during the tenth century is considered below, but the origins of the Midland shires are generally attributed to the English kings of this period and to the succeeding century. The East Midland counties of Lincoln, Nottingham, Derby and Leicester took their names from four of the Danish Five Boroughs, or *fifburgingas*; the fifth Borough, Stamford, lies in Lincolnshire. These Danish towns served as central nodes for their respective shires, whilst each held an important position amongst the confederation which existed prior to the West Saxon re-conquest.

In the West and South Midlands, shires were organised around newly built fortified towns or re-fortified centres, with the shires taking the names of the settlements. These 'new' shires were remarkably regular in form with their dependant towns nearly always centrally placed. Examples include Stafford, Hereford, Worcester, Warwick, Oxford, Northampton, Bedford, Gloucester and Buckingham. It seems that the West Saxon system of shires, as planted in the midlands, was developed as part of a programme of military organisation based upon hinterlands supplying the men and resources for their upkeep. The dating of the Midland shires is problematic but some scholars have recently argued that the powerful Ealdorman Eadric Streona created them all as one administrative measure in 1007.

As Henry Loyn has observed, the shiring pattern to the north of a line stretching from the Mersey to the Humber is less compact then that of the Midlands and Wessex. The former kingdom of Northumbria passed back into English hands after 954 with York as its obvious administrative centre. Both Yorkshire and Lincolnshire, to the south, were subdivided into three parts or 'ridings', again, probably for the purposes of military and financial organisation. Loyn has noted that the substantial districts north of the Humber in Late Anglo-Saxon times are better viewed as ealdormanries, whereas, in the south, an *ealdorman* would administer several shires. Either way, the two systems have much in common with regard to the mechanics of local governance and these are considered below.

Hundreds and estates

The hundred was the basic unit of local governance from at least the tenth century when it is first mentioned explicitly in a document of King Edgar's reign (957–975) known as the Hundred Ordinance.

The Ordinance clearly requires men to attend the hundred courts on a regular basis and, through its business, a series of public duties were organised. Amongst these was the raising of a posse to pursue cattle thieves with careful arrangements in place with regard to intra-hundredal jurisdiction. The Ordinance warrants quotation in full to give a sense of the fundamental role played by the institution:

> This is the ordinance on how the hundred shall be held:
>
> **1.** First, that they are to assemble every four weeks and each man is to do justice to another.
> **2.** If the need is urgent, then one is to inform the man in charge of the hundred, and he then the men over the tithings; and all are to go forth,

where God may guide them that they may reach [the thief]. Justice is to be done on the thief as it was Edmunds decree previously.

2.1. And the value of the stolen property is to be given to him who owns the cattle, and the rest is to be divided into two, half for the hundred and half for the lord — except the men; and the lord is to succeed to the men.

3. And the man who neglects this and opposes the decision of the hundred — and afterwards that charge is proved against him — is to pay thirty pence to the hundred, and on a second occasion sixty pence, half to the hundred, half to the lord.

3.1. If he does it a third time, he is to pay half a pound; at the fourth time he is to forfeit all that he owns and be an outlaw, unless the king allows him [to remain in] the land.

4. And we decreed concerning strange cattle, that no one was to keep any, unless he have the witness of the man in charge of the hundred or of the man over the tithing; and he [the witness] is to be very trustworthy.

4.1. And unless he has one of them, he is not to be allowed to vouch to warranty.

5. Further, we decreed, if one hundred follows up a trail into another hundred, that is to be made known to the man in charge of that hundred, and he is then to go with them.

5.1 And if he neglects it, he is to pay thirty shillings to the king.

6. If anyone evades the law and flees, he who supported him in that injury is to pay the simple compensation (the value of the goods).

6.1. And if he is accused of abetting his escape, he is to clear himself according as it is established in the district.

7. In the hundred, as in any other court, it is our will that in every suit the common law be enjoined, and a day appointed when it shall be carried out..

7.1. And he who fails to appear on the appointed day — unless it is through his lords summons — is to pay thirty shillings compensation, and on a fixed day perform what he should have done before.

The basic functions of the West Saxon hundredal unit can all be found as features of the landscape prior to the tenth century and it appears likely that earlier social and political institutions were re-shuffled at this time. It is evident that the entire administrative machine was tightened up and regularised from the reign of Alfred, but increasingly so during the tenth-century reigns of kings such as Edward the Elder (899–925), Athelstan and Edgar.

In the Danelaw areas the equivalent unit to the hundred was the wapentake (**25**). The word 'wapentake' is derived from the Old Norse *vapnatak*, which refers to the brandishing of weapons in consent at an assembly.

Meeting places are attested prior to the tenth century, such as the *gemot beorh*, or 'meeting mound' incorporated into a description of the bounds of a estate at Calbourne on the Isle of Wight in 826, but we know little about the composition or remit of these early assemblies. Once the earliest Anglo-Saxons had organised themselves into identifiable

25 *Hundreds and wapentakes: the terminology of administrative units in Wessex and the Danelaw.* Redrawn from Hill 1981

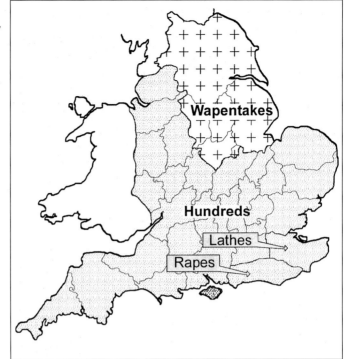

groups, so the process of kingdom building began. Whilst small kin based groups might rely on infrequent group meetings to settle disputes and make decisions affecting the folk, larger territories expanded often by violent conquest will have required more formal assemblies from an early stage.

The earliest documentary reference to an assembly with administrative responsibility is recorded in the later seventh-century laws attributed to the Kentish kings Hlothere (673–85) and Eadric (685–6). The earliest documentary evidence for *public* assembly, however, comes from a charter of Coenwulf, king of Mercia (796–821), dated 801, which describes how an estate has been freed from the burden of *popularia concilia*. King Offa (757–96) had previously granted the estate in question in 767, presumably with the burden, and the Coenwulf charter was appended to the original. As noted above, however, public assemblies are likely to have been a requirement from the earliest period of stable settlement in post-Roman England. The evidence of place-names lends further weight to the antiquity of the function and this aspect is considered below.

The developed hundredal system of Late Anglo-Saxon Wessex shows features that suggest considerable antiquity, perhaps not always the hundred area itself, as described by its presently observed boundaries but more probably in the location and nature of its meeting places and their names. As noted above, the naming of certain hundreds is archaic in character, which has led some to suggest a pagan origin for their use as folk meeting-places. Names suggestive of pre-Christian activity include those referring to the heads of animals on stakes. Manshead Hundred in Bedfordshire means literally that — although the name might refer either to a 'head' or 'compliment' of people at a public meeting just as easily as it might record a displayed human head (itself a powerful symbol of judicial authority). Names such as 'Swineshead' it can be argued, represented just that; either a pig's head or a carved representation placed as a notable mark in the landscape. Audrey Meaney has recently considered hundred meeting-places, which were traditionally open-air sites, and noted that the earliest examples might be those in isolated locations, where the hundred has taken its name from the meeting-place. There are a few examples of apparently tribal names incorporated into hundred names, for example, Hurstingstone Hundred in Huntingdonshire translates as 'stone of the Hyrstingas', recalling the terminology of the Tribal Hidage.

The choice of sites for hundred meeting-places is a subject of considerable interest. Bridges, fords and crossroads seem to reflect purely practical choices based on the need for a dispersed population to meet at a commonly known point in the landscape. Examples include the Hundreds of Kingsbridge, Wiltshire, Armingford, Cambridgeshire and Normancross, Huntingdonshire. Of greater interest, particularly to archaeologists, are the sites that make use of physical features in the landscape. Meeting-places often made use of natural features such as stones or hillocks, although many sites are known which incorporated either a manmade mound or a standing stone. It is possible, and some might argue probable, that the Anglo-Saxons were not able to distinguish between manmade and natural features. In this respect, one must be wary of the tendency to ascribe an Anglo-Saxon origin for features described using the Old English terms for mounds, *beorg* and *hlaew* (modern 'barrow' and 'low' or 'lew'). Indeed, the Anglo-Saxons used *beorg* to refer to any type of eminence ranging from a minor barrow to the Alps. These reservations aside, there are many known hundred meeting-places that utilised physical features of human origin. The use of stones is recorded in hundred names such as Cuttlestone, or 'Cuthwulf's stone', Staffordshire and Kinwardstone, or 'Cyneweard's stone', Wiltshire.

The use of mounds is widespread and archaeology has made a valuable contribution to our understanding of these sites. Barrows such as the meeting-place of Wormelow Hundred, Herefordshire are usually presumed to be mounds of prehistoric origin. The excavation of a meeting mound at Milton Keynes, the meeting-place of Secklow Hundred led to an examination of records of excavations at other meeting mounds in England. The Secklow mound is the only one excavated to date with an awareness of the potential of the intervention beyond the possibility of recovering valuable finds form burials. The excavation work showed that the mound was purpose built and further research showed that out of twelve further excavated mounds, only one proved to be of prehistoric origin. Undoubtedly, many meeting mounds are of prehistoric origin, but the construction of mounds for the purposes of public meetings during the Christian period is of particular interest.

Besides archaeological possibilities with regard to the dating of deliberately built mounds, it might be possible to suggest that mounds of known origin were necessary after the conversion to Christianity, when documentary sources indicate an increasing suspicion of mounds either known or suspected to contain burials.

The majority of our evidence for the names of hundreds is, however, derived from Domesday Book, by which time a significant number of hundreds held their meetings at

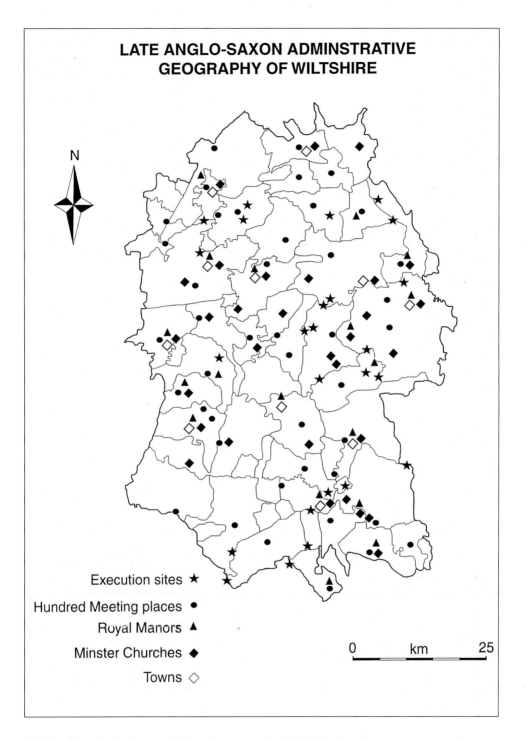

26 *The Late Anglo-Saxon administrative geography of Wiltshire showing royal manors, minster churches, hundred meeting-places, towns and execution cemeteries in relation to hundred boundaries.* Redrawn from Reynolds 1998

the hundredal manor from which they took their name. It seems likely that the traditional meeting places for these latter sites have been lost.

The elements which constituted the instruments of secular and religious jurisdiction within individual hundreds ideally comprised a royal estate centre, or *villa regalis*, a meeting place where hundredal affairs were conducted, a minster or superior church, a market place and a judicial execution cemetery. Through these agencies the network of agricultural estates and their inhabitants was tied in all aspects into a kingdom-wide system of governance. The distribution of these administrative features in the county of Wiltshire is shown in (**26**); note the stunningly central location of the meeting places of the northern hundreds. Some have suggested that meeting-places were located on boundaries without exploring the status of the particular boundaries in question. Whilst a meeting mound mentioned in an Anglo-Saxon estate survey, or one located by a modern place-name or physical feature, might lay upon an estate boundary, it is its positioning within the hundredal unit which is significant. It might be argued that the central placing of the meeting-place within a hundredal unit in fact pre-dates many of the small estates that came about through the fragmentation of larger units in the tenth century. Meeting places on mere estate boundaries, therefore, are perhaps better seen as having been incorporated into the boundaries of new estates. This proposition agrees with the modern view of barrows, including those containing Early Anglo-Saxon interments, found on estate boundaries; that they have simply been incorporated as convenient markers into the perimeters of Late Anglo-Saxon land units.

Meeting places located on the boundaries of hundreds or even shires might reflect the increased importance of such sites. The shire courts, which met only twice a year, were substantial meetings that dealt with major lawsuits and such sites were often located upon important boundaries. The Iron Age hillfort at Wandlebury near Cambridge, lies on a boundary between two hundreds and is recorded as the site of two major assemblies between the late tenth century and the mid-eleventh century. The latter meeting was known as the 'assembly of the nine shires' and judicial functions are perhaps borne out by the finding of unusual burials at the site, perhaps the bodies of executed criminals. The locations of execution burials on the whole, however, suggests that capital punishments were enacted at locations away from hundred meeting-places; perhaps the magnitude of cases heard at the shire court necessitated punishment in view of the shire. The shire court for Berkshire was held at *cwicelmeshlæw* (Cwichelm's barrow) which can be visited today adjacent to the Ridgeway near the village of East Hendred (now in Oxfordshire)(**colour plate 1**).

Nominally, the hundred literally comprised one hundred hides of land. The variation in size of the Wessex hundreds clearly indicates that hidage assessments do not relate to geographical extent, although one must also take into account the existence of so-called half-, double- and triple-hundreds. Only a few fragments of written evidence exist which throw light on the potential complexities of hundredal organisation but the general impression given is one of uniformly organised, if not regularly sized, territories.

In the Danelaw areas, both the shire and hundredal geography is far more regular than in Wessex. The problems surrounding this observation have been outlined above, but it cannot be doubted that the majority of the Danelaw shires and their accompanying sub-

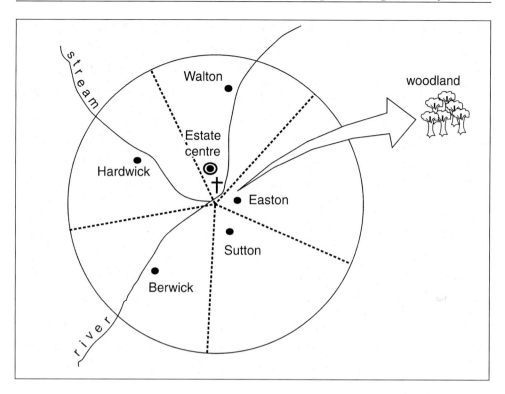

27 *A model reconstruction of a multiple estate showing specialised settlements and their relationship to an estate centre with a royal manor and a minster church*

districts are late creations in comparison to their West Saxon counterparts — whatever the precise chronology.

Agricultural estates

Agricultural estates were the most basic units in the Anglo-Saxon landscape. The use of the hide as a measurement by Bede and by the compilers of the Tribal Hidage suggests that the extent of individual homesteads could be well defined. The organisation of groups of estates in the Middle Anglo-Saxon period, however, is difficult to understand, although a number of theories have been advanced, most importantly the concept of the 'multiple estate'.

Prior to the tenth century, the landscape was characterised by large estates under royal or ecclesiastical ownership. It appears that within these estates individual farmsteads or small farming settlements specialised in the production of certain produce or stock. Each of these settlements was responsible to an estate centre for the purposes of administration and taxation (**27**). The evidence of place-names is an important source for the model reconstruction of the types of settlements that multiple estates contained. Names ending in *wic*, in a rural context, apparently refer to farmsteads or places of production. Hardwick

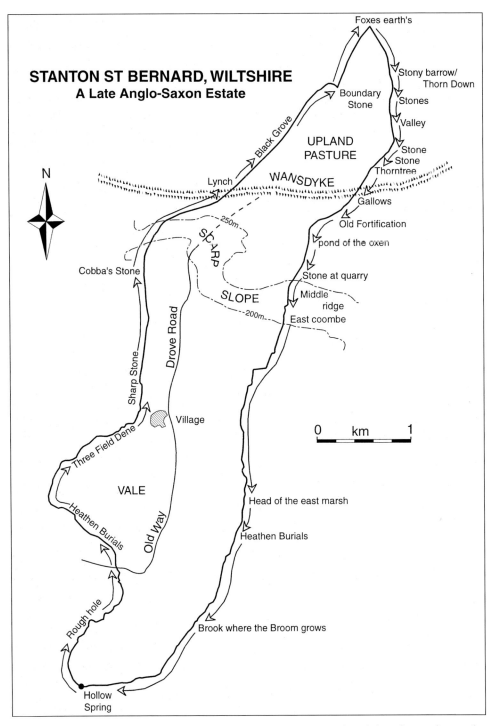

28 *The bounds of the Late Anglo-Saxon estate at Stanton St Bernard, Wiltshire from a charter of AD957. Although the boundary marks describe the limits of the land unit, it is still possible to gain an insight into the internal structure and function of the estate*

or 'sheep-farm' is a common place-name and belongs to a group of names that record settlements with a specialised economic base. Further obvious examples include Cowick, Devon, Oxwick, Norfolk and Woolwich, Kent. Less obvious place-names include the widely attested Berwick, or 'barley farm', Chiswick, or 'cheese farm', Middlesex, Spitchwick, or 'bacon farm', Devon and Bewick, or 'bee farm' in the East Riding of Yorkshire. Place-names such as Westwick, Eastwick and Middlewick, or Norton, Sutton, Weston and Easton provide additional evidence for the former existence of an estate centre with small dependant farms denoted by their geographical relationship to the head manor. Further names such as Aisholt, or, 'ash wood' in Somerset and Akeley, or 'oak wood' in Buckinghamshire provide evidence for the natural resource base of the Anglo-Saxon landscape. There is good evidence, however, to indicate that woodland resources far from the estate centre might be exploited.

Della Hooke has suggested that an element of the hundredal geography of tenth-century and later England may have been based upon pre-existing multiple estates. Research into the Hampshire evidence has led Eric Klingelhöfer to propose what he has termed 'archaic hundreds' located in river valleys, which were the precursors to the hundreds of the tenth century and later.

Detailed boundary clauses are rare prior to the tenth century and the earlier surviving sets are in Latin with relatively few boundary marks recorded. An exception to the rule is the authentic bounds of Little Bedwyn in East Wiltshire, dated 778. Although the boundary clause is both early and in Latin, the bounds are as detailed as any later set. The need for the Bedwyn estate to have been described so precisely at such an early date suggests that similarly well-defined units existed in the surrounding landscape. One might expect an isolated estate carved out of a larger territory to have simplified boundaries if it had no neighbours.

During the tenth century a process that has become known as 'estate fragmentation' occurred in many regions. Former multiple estates became subdivided by grants of land from the king to the church, but also to private individuals. The basis of the modern pattern of parish boundaries was established, or at least largely fossilised, at this time and it is commonly the case that the larger modern parishes were formerly royal lands or the property of minster churches.

The boundary clauses of Anglo-Saxon charters are the principal source for reconstructing the nature of rural estates on the ground. Boundary surveyors often incorporated a range of features related to the agricultural base of the estate and the bounds of Stanton St Bernard in Wiltshire are given here as a model example (**28**). The Stanton estate boundary is recorded in three authentic sets of bounds of 905, 957 and 960. There are minor changes in the details recorded by each set of bounds, but for our purposes the 957 bounds will suffice. The grant itself was one of twenty hides from King Eadwig (955–9) to Oswulf, Bishop. In common with other land charters of the Later Anglo-Saxon period, the bounds are written in Old English:

> First to the Hollow Spring — to the Rough Hole — then to the Old Way —
> to the heathen burials — then to three-field Dean — from the Dean to the
> Sharp Stone — then to Cobba's Stone — from the stone to a Row [of trees]

by a Lynch till it comes to Black Groves — then to the Boundary stone — from the stone to the Foxes' Earth's' — then to the Stony Barrow on Thorn Down approaching it from the north — From the Barrow to the Stones along the Dean going downwards — from the Stone to a Stone — then to a Thorn-tree — then to the wrongdoers gallows on Wansdyke — then to the Old Fortification, meeting it on the middle of one side — from the Fortification to the Pond of the Oxen — then there lies a Stone at a Quarry — from the Stone to the Middle Ridge to East Combe — then to the Head of the East Marsh to the Heathen Burials — to the Brook where the Broom grows — then along the stream once more to Hollow Spring.

The range of landscape features incorporated into the Stanton bounds gives a good impression of the way in which estates were laid out with respect to resource availability. The boundary clause describes fields (Old English 'open country'), including, perhaps, lynchets, or cultivation terraces, water sources, a quarry, an execution site and a watering place (**colour plate 2**). The Stanton estate encompasses a varied topography in common with neighbouring estates on the northern edge of the Vale of Pewsey in Wiltshire. Each estate comprises a settlement zone on the clay vale with specialised and pastoral requirements met by the scarp-slope and upland parts of the land unit (**colour plate 3**) which were accessed by drove roads (**colour plate 4**) leading from the settlement.

Clearly not every agricultural estate had access to the full range of resources necessary for the support of the estate and this factor probably goes some way to explaining the curious occurrence of detached parts of parishes often observed in later sources. Indeed, a glance at county maps of the nineteenth century will often reveal detached parts of parishes lying in adjoining counties.

The development of open-field agriculture seems to have taken place from the tenth century in the Midland and surrounding counties. The communal necessities of such an agricultural system fostered the development of nucleated villages in these regions. In the upland regions and in areas such as Norfolk, settlement patterns remained largely dispersed.

It is clear that by the time of the Norman Conquest there was precious little but points of terminology to distinguish between Late Anglo-Saxon and Norman social and economic circumstances.

Civil Defence

As noted in the preceding chapters, military service and military obligations were based on hidage assessments. Before the late ninth century, the historical and place-name sources provide the greater part of the evidence for the existence of military organisation. There is archaeological evidence from the Kingdom of Mercia for fortified settlements, or early towns, at Hereford (which literally means 'army-ford') in the late eighth century and, perhaps, at Tamworth at about the same time. The most impressive legacy of Mercian defensive capabilities, however, is Offa's Dyke, the great linear earthwork that divided the Mercians from the Welsh. The frontier stretched from the Dee Estuary in the north, down to the Severn Estuary, and serves to illustrate the considerable power exercised by King Offa in late eighth-century Mercia. The surviving earthwork is not continuous and certain parts have been slighted. David Hill's work on the Dyke has suggested that the earthwork was built in stretches, utilising the system of military obligations to muster labour and resources.

The earthworks known as east and west Wansdyke (**colour plate 5**), in the counties of Wiltshire and Somerset, perhaps represent unfinished public works of Middle Anglo-Saxon date; the result of a short-lived settlement between the West Saxons and the Mercians in the late eighth or early ninth century. The ditch of both sections of the earthwork faces northward indicating that its builders were based to the south. Traditionally both east and west Wansdyke are dated to the late- or sub-Roman period. In the absence of secure archaeological dating, however, such a programme of defensive activity fits rather more comfortably into a Middle Anglo-Saxon context, as Wessex's equivalent to Offa's Dyke.

Grants of land by royal charter increasingly reserved three obligations from the grantee of an estate from an early period. These obligations, otherwise known as the *Trinoda Necessitas*, from a forged Canterbury charter of the late tenth century, comprised bridge-work, fortress-work and military service. Nicholas Brooks has noted a steady increase in the number of charters reserving the three burdens from the beginning of the ninth century, but of the surviving charters dating to between 750 and 850 less than one fifth record them. A charter of King Cenwulf of Mercia of about 800 records that only five men were required from an estate of 30 hides when the *fyrd* (the army) was called out. Later on, in Wessex, the situation as it related to Berkshire is detailed in a Domesday Book entry relating to that shire. The passage records that 'If the king sent an army anywhere, only one soldier went from five hides, and four shillings were given him from each hide as subsistence and wages for two months. This money, indeed, was not sent to the king but was given to the soldiers'. Based on the fact that Berkshire hides appear to have been much smaller than their counterparts elsewhere in Wessex, Sir Frank Stenton has argued for a much higher *fyrd* assessment.

It seems that those who fought or served under such terms were part of a select *fyrd* comprising well-equipped and well-trained warriors, each supported by his home estate, which he might own or at least part own. The armies of the later Anglo-Saxon period appear largely professional, although the kings retained their right to call on the general population to aid the defence of the realm.

Coastal defence and the provision of ships for the navy were additional obligations that befell inland rural estates as well as those actually located at strategic points along the coastline. In 1008, for example, the *Anglo-Saxon Chronicle* annal relates how 'the king ordered that they should determinedly build ships all over England: that is, one warship from three hundred and ten hides, and from eight hides a helmet and mailcoat'. The birth of the English navy, however, is commonly attributed to the reign of Alfred and an oft' quoted passage from the Chronicle under the year 897. In order to deal with the threat of Viking warships 'King Alfred ordered long-ships to be built to oppose the 'askrs' (warships); they were well-nigh twice as long as the others, some had sixty oars, some more; they were both swifter and steadier, and also more responsive than the others; they

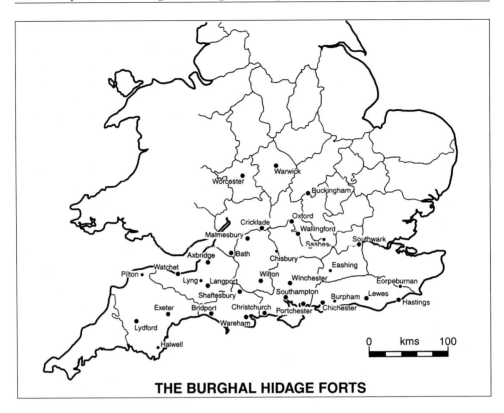

29 *The forts of the Burghal Hidage.* Redrawn from Hill 1981

were neither of Frisian design nor of Danish, but as it seemed to himself that they might be most useful'. Five hide units could expect to send a man to either the army or the navy, but never both under normal circumstances.

Civil defence: the burhs

The origins of the Anglo-Saxon public *burh* lie in the turbulent period of the late ninth and earlier tenth centuries. Alfred's defeat and subsequent settlement with the Danish army in 878 led, as we have seen, to the partition of England into the West Saxon kingdom and the Danelaw. Alfred initiated the building of a series of fortified places, some containing markets, minster churches and royal accommodation, others were re-fortified centres of Roman origin, whereas the so-called 'emergency burhs' were lesser fortifications apparently used on a periodic or insubstantial basis. Alfred died in 899 to be succeeded by his son Edward the Elder, who went on to lead a successful campaign of reconquest of the Danelaw. Edward built many new *burhs*, whose dates of construction or rebuilding are noted in *Anglo-Saxon Chronicle* entries, particularly of the second decade of the tenth century. The social and economic aspects of the *burhs* are considered in Chapter 5.

The earliest West Saxon *burhs* lay in the kingdom's heartland and these can be plotted onto a map (**29**) using a remarkable document known as the *burghal hidage*. In essence, the *burghal hidage* is a list of 33 major fortifications giving details about the number of hides belonging to each place. The relevance of the hidage assessments is crucial to our understanding of the way in which the burghal forts were supported by military obligations of estates within their remit. After listing the series of forts, the burghal hidage ends with a note describing how:

> 'For the maintenance and defence of an acre's breadth of wall sixteen hides are required. If every hide is represented by one man, then every pole *(an Anglo-Saxon system of measurement)* of wall can be manned by four men. Then for the maintenance of twenty poles of wall eighty hides are required'.

Armed with this formula it is possible to reconstruct the length of burghal defences at each of the recorded sites in the early tenth century. As many scholars have observed, and as might be expected, there is often a close correlation between the tenth-century defences and those attested on the ground by various means, such as archaeological and topographical studies.

The *burghal hidage* list survives in a sixteenth-century copy of an eleventh-century text from Winchester, but also in several other post-conquest documents. In common with the Tribal Hidage, the possibility exists that the Burghal Hidage incorporates material from several different sources. Compilation of the document is traditionally dated to between 911–14 on the basis that certain other known Anglo-Saxon *burhs* were either not included in the list, having later origins, or were known to have come under the control of the West Saxon kings at a known date. Oxford, for example, passed into the hands of Edward the Elder upon the death of the Mercian Ealdorman Aethelred in 911. The *burh* at Buckingham, on the other hand, which is also mentioned in the *burghal hidage*, is noted in the *Anglo-Saxon Chronicle*, which refers to its construction under the year 914. It is recorded that 'King Edward went to Buckingham with his army, and stayed there four weeks, and made both the boroughs, on each side of the river, before he went away.' It is likely, then, that the compilation of the *burghal hidage* took place at some time between 911, when Oxford came into West Saxon hands, and 914, when the *burh* at Buckingham was built, but the list itself may be based on earlier material.

Each of the burghal hidage forts was located no more than forty miles from the next, which represents a comprehensive and centrally planned exercise only achievable through a powerful and efficient system of governance and administration. The distribution of the forts is remarkably even, although concern was clearly directed to providing a line of frontier forts sited upon the northern boundaries of Somerset (Bath), Wiltshire (Malmesbury, Cricklade and Chisbury), Berkshire (Oxford, Wallingford and Sashes) and Surrey (Southwark). The western part of this frontier line had been of significance to the West Saxons since the later eighth and early ninth centuries, when Berkshire came into being and when the West Saxons had regained North Wiltshire from the Mercians to the north.

The coastal *burhs*, such as Watchet, Somerset, Bridport and Wareham in Dorset and Portchester Castle, Hampshire had an obvious motivation; to keep a watch for sea-borne raiders. The inland *burhs* were either existing settlements of economic and political importance, such as Winchester or they were among the smaller forts with much lower hidages to support them. The comparative areas and topographical characteristics of the burghal hidage forts are shown below following Martin Biddle's 1976 classification based on a division between burghal towns that served a whole range of functions and burghal forts.

Burghal Towns

Reused Roman walled towns

Winchester	2400 hides
Chichester	1500 hides
Bath	1000 hides
Exeter	734 hides

New towns on open sites (rectangular perimeter)

Wallingford	2400 hides
Wareham	1600 hides
Cricklade	1500 hides
Oxford	1400 hides

New towns on promontory sites (irregular perimeter)

Wilton	1400 hides
Lewes	1300 hides
Malmesbury	1200 hides
Bridport	760 hides
Shaftesbury	700 hides
Langport	600 hides
Watchet	513 hides
Twyneham	470 hides
Axebridge	400 hides
Lydford	140 hides
Lyng	100 hides

Burghal forts

Re-used Iron Age or Roman forts

Chisbury	700 hides
Hastings	500 hides
Portchester	500 hides
Pilton	360 hides
Halwell	300 hides
Southampton	150 hides

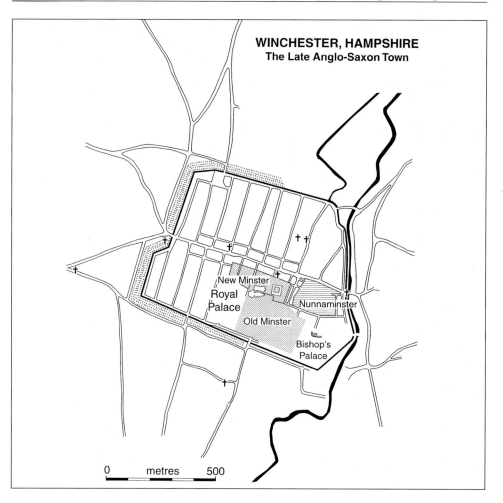

30 *Winchester in the Late Anglo-Saxon period. Note the regularity of the street pattern within the walls.* Redrawn from Ottaway 1992

New forts

Sashes	1000 hides
Burpham	720 hides
Eashing	600 hides
Eortheburnan	324 hides
Southwark	1800 hides

Besides the landscape context of the *burghal hidage* forts, their form and layout is also indicative of centralised planning. Our understanding of the layout and nature of West Saxon *burhs* has been well served by the efforts of archaeologists. Here, the examples of Winchester, Oxford and Chisbury, together with reference to other sites, will serve to illustrate the layout of a Roman walled town, a classic newly-planned *burh* and an 'emergency *burh*'. The newly-founded sites are of particular interest as they provide models of the Anglo-Saxon concept of a fortified settlement. *Burhs* that made use of earlier fortifications such as Roman walls or Iron Age hillforts were of a largely predetermined form as their defensive circuits matched existing features at their respective sites. Similarly, a significant group of newly built promontory forts also had their plan-forms largely determined by their topographical locations.

Former Roman walled towns incorporated into the burghal hidage include Winchester, Exeter, Chichester and Bath retained the basic alignment of their original major thoroughfares, a factor due more to the location of gateways rather than any desire to revive the Roman road system within the walls. Prior to Martin Biddle's work at Winchester, it was thought that the town's gridded street system was of Roman origin. At Trafalgar Street, a coin of Alfred was found in a deposit below the earliest street surface, and a coin of the early tenth century was found lying on the top of the second surface. Archaeological excavation elsewhere in the city has shown that where they are found, the earliest street surfaces are of consistent appearance. There was an intra-mural street running around the circuit of the walls, so as to allow access along the entire wall. The High Street frontages ran east to west between each of the major gateways, while access roads to the rear of the High Street properties ran parallel to the main street. A series of lanes ran both north and south from the High Street and these were laid out with astonishing order, being a regular 16 poles apart (about 5m). The regularity of the grid itself provides strong evidence to support the contention that the layout of Winchester at the time of the burghal hidage, was the result of one co-ordinated exercise (**30**).

Anglo-Saxon activity at Oxford is first attested by the founding of St Frideswide's Monastery in 727. The burghal town however, was laid out in one exercise furnished with gridded streets, gates and substantial defences in about 890, incorporating the precinct of the monastery (**31**). There are good grounds to support the contention that Oxford was a Mercian foundation, probably of Æthelflæd 'Lady of the Mercians' and not one of Alfred's forts. Oxford seems to have been a mint, in common with Winchester, from about 900, or perhaps as early as 890.

The town itself was laid out with two principal streets forming a crossroads in the centre of the fortified area. A number of minor streets are known to have existed in the northern part of the town and the existence of yet more within the rest of the area is likely. The four entrances necessitated by the principal roads were located broadly on the points of the compass. The earliest metalling of the internal road system has been examined in a few locations. The discovery that they are of uniform grade, and the presence of an open drain (called the 'kennel'), along the high street are good examples of 'administrative archaeology'. Although the defences of the town are established with a degree of certainty, there is discrepancy whereby the hidage assessment of 1,300 falls 163 hides short of the estimated actual length of the ramparts.

The ramparts of the *burh* have been explored by archaeological excavation on the northern side of the city. Timber posts, set just under 2m apart, held back earth dug from a ditch whose near edge lay some 3m from the revetment. Planks were set on edge against the inside edge of the posts with the earth piled behind. Alluvial clay and lacing timbers were used to strengthen the rampart, but early in the tenth century an outward

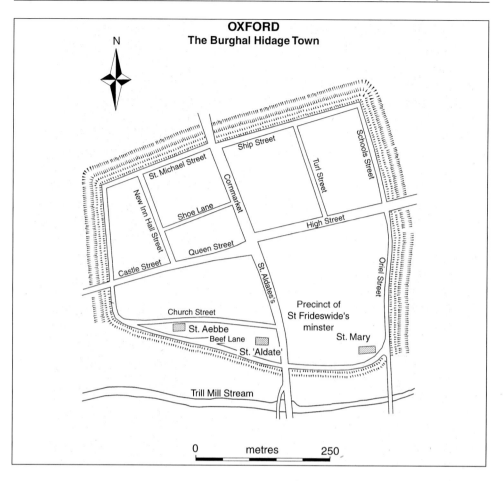

31 *The Burghal Hidage fort at Oxford showing the defensive circuit and rectilinear street pattern laid out c. AD 890.* Redrawn from Blair 1994

ragstone revetment was added. John Blair has noted that Oxford with its stone outer walls would have presented a formidable sight to the inhabitants of the Upper Thames region, which had seen nothing of a comparable nature since the demise of Roman Dorchester and Alchester.

Chisbury hillfort lies on the eastern edge of the county of Wiltshire within a short distance of the boundary with Berkshire. The site comprises a small multi-vallate hillfort of late Iron Age construction (first century BC). There are problems with the firm identification of the site as that mentioned in the burghal hidage. The major reservation is that the defences of the fort based on an assessment of 700 hides give a measurement of 880m, whereas the hillfort ramparts stretch in reality to 994m. The site deserves serious consideration nevertheless, for there is a masonry chapel at the east entrance; a common feature at other burhs including Oxford and Wareham. There is current debate, however, about the dating of chapels at the gates of forts and it remains a possibility that such buildings are no earlier than the eleventh century. At Wareham the hidage assessment related only to the earthen fortifications on three sides of the settlement and did not include the length of riverbank on the south side, whilst Wallingford's river frontage was included in the circuit. Such variations show that it was possible for the length of assessed defences not to correspond with the total extent of the limits of the fort. If Chisbury hillfort is to be equated with the *Cissanbyrig* listed in the burghal hidage, then its position in the landscape can only be described as stunning. The site offers extensive views in all directions and was ideally sited to communicate with other defensive sites by the use of a beacon or other such means. The interior of the fort is largely unoccupied, but there are no features to suggest occupation or planning of the interior. It seems likely that Chisbury was similar to the fort at Burpham in Sussex in that periodic occupation took place as opposed to any concerted move toward urban development. Without archaeological fieldwork, however, the firm identification of Chisbury must remain in question.

Under the entry for 915, the year succeeding the building of Buckingham, the *Anglo-Saxon Chronicle* relates how 'King Edward went with his army to Bedford…stayed four weeks, and before he went away ordered the borough on the south side of the river to be built.' The fortifications built by Edward the Elder, largely after the compilation of the *burghal hidage*, represent an impressive campaign of civil defence, especially when added to the existing chain of forts first established in the reign of his father, King Alfred. In addition to Buckingham and Bedford, Edward either erected or refurbished a formidable number of *burhs* in eastern and northern England. Examples include Witham (912), Maldon (916) Colchester (917), Essex, *Wigingamere* (perhaps Wing in Buckinghamshire)(917), Towcester, Northamptonshire (917), Manchester (919) and Nottingham (920), among others.

If a *burh* could indeed be built from scratch in a period of about four weeks, a further impression of the efficiency of Late Anglo-Saxon military institutions can be gained. The building of a fort or the refurbishment of existing defences would have required considerable resources in terms of human labour, but also with respect to timber, or perhaps stone, which were used as materials for the construction of ramparts. After the setting out and digging of a defensive ditch, the work of carpenters and masons would have begun. The building of palisades and fortified gates would have required particular skill, but the system of military obligations in place by the late ninth and early tenth centuries was clearly capable of mustering the necessary workforce, expertise and resources.

Civil defence in the localities: communications, beacons and bell-towers

The evidence for local systems of civil defence is buried within the place-name record, a range of historical sources, especially charters, and to a limited extent in the archaeological record. For the local networks, there is nothing to compare with the burghal hidage in terms of detail, but modern archaeological studies are just beginning to reveal the potential of archaeological approaches to the subject. The preliminary results of one such project, in the Avebury region of North Wiltshire are presented below.

32 *A reconstruction of the firing of a late Anglo-Saxon signalling beacon warning of an approaching Viking army.* Drawn by Sarah Semple

The village of Yatesbury in Wiltshire lies some 3.5km to the north west of the famous prehistoric monument at Avebury. Research excavations at Yatesbury throughout the 1990s revealed a series of archaeological features that are best seen as part of a late Anglo-Saxon localised early warning system. Among the archaeological features that have been investigated is an earthwork enclosure measuring just less than 200m in diameter with a Late Anglo-Saxon phase. It is possible that this earthwork is that from which the village takes its name. The place-name Yatesbury may well equate to Old English burh-gate, the fortified structure mentioned in the *Geþyncðo* as a requirement of *thegnly* status.

A reconstruction of the Late Anglo-Saxon road system, based on the finding of a south entrance to the Yatesbury enclosure, and upon place-name evidence, has suggested that a *herepað*, or 'army road' ran through the site linking it with Avebury. Remarkable evidence to further strengthen the likelihood that Yatesbury played a significant local role in civil defence, was recovered during exploratory excavations on a turf-built mound of Early Bronze Age origin (*c*.2000BC), which was located on the western edge of the enclosure noted above. After the removal of the modern turf, cleaning of the underlying surface revealed that it had been thoroughly burnt by an intense fire. Initially, it was thought that either recent burning or perhaps prehistoric activity might be held to account for this. The digging of a cutting on the south side of the mound, however, revealed part of a ditch of 'V'-shaped section, apparently running around the summit describing an enclosed area of some 10m in diameter. The filling of the ditch was composed of two thick bands of charcoal rich soil. The burning activity can be dated to *c.*1000 on the basis of a large, freshly broken, rim-sherd, decorated with wheel-stamps, found at the bottom of the ditch (**colour plate 6**).

It seems reasonable to interpret the charcoal ditch-fills as sweepings from a beacon platform (**32**), itself located on the edge of a defensible enclosure astride a *herepað* route. The place-name evidence for the existence of a *herepað* comes from Avebury, where the principal axes of Anglo-Saxon passage through the monument was east to west and not north to south as it is today. A clear impression of the early alignment can be gained by standing in front of the Red Lion public house facing south, and looking from left to right. Early documents refer to the henge monument at Avebury as *waledic*, or 'ditch of the Britons', whereas the place-name itself most likely means '*burh* by the Avon'. Archaeological excavations from the 1960s have shown that the Middle and Late Anglo-Saxon settlement lay outside the west entrance of the monument, but an analysis of earthworks and other evidence has revealed a regular apparently planned layout with a central street within a circuit of defences. The parish church occupies just under a quarter of the total area and was most likely of minster status in the Late Anglo-Saxon period, with notable surviving features. Although Avebury and Yatesbury were joined by road, they are not intervisible, which necessitates an intermediate point of sight. This role is more than adequately performed by Silbury Hill (**colour plate 7**) whose summit has been shown by archaeological excavation to have been fortified with a timber palisade giving the top of the mound its step-like profile. The finding of a coin of King Æthelred the Unready of 'about AD 1010' provides a date for the defences, which is corroborated by the revised dating of a horse-bit found on the summit in the eighteenth century as an eleventh-century piece.

The name Silbury is best interpreted as 'hall-burh' and no-doubt records the former presence of the fort. The prominence of Silbury as an earthwork probably meant that it served a much wider purpose than simply providing a link between Avebury and Yatesbury, including keeping watch over the Bath to London Roman road. In fact, the Yatesbury to Avebury *herepað* can be traced as a route describing the Marlborough Downs area, which was ultimately spurred into parts of the Roman road network which were still in use. Military roads are common features in charter bounds and the case study given above suggests that some importance was placed upon parallel means of communication; roads and beacons.

The *Anglo-Saxon Chronicle* records Viking activity in the Avebury region in both 1006 and 1010. At the latter date the Vikings are recorded as close-by as Cannings Marsh where they 'burned it all.' It seems probable that the Avebury/Yatesbury system played a part in the English defence of the area, although it appears to have failed on this occasion as the chronicle notes subsequently in the same entry that the marauders 'had gone as far as they wanted'.

33 *A reconstruction of the Anglo-Saxon network of beacons in Hampshire.* Redrawn from Hill 1997

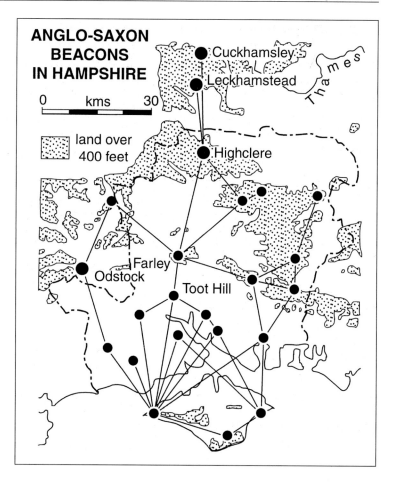

ANGLO-SAXON BEACONS IN HAMPSHIRE

0   kms   30

land over 400 feet

Cuckhamsley
Leckhamstead
Highclere
Farley
Odstock
Toot Hill

David Hill has recently set out the evidence for an Anglo-Saxon beacon system throughout southern England. A number of largely tenth-century charter bounds record *weard-setl* (place where guard is kept), *weardan hyll* (beacon hill), *weard-dun* (beacon hill) and *weard-stall* (guardhouse). The adjoining estates of Highclere and Burghclere in Hampshire are defined by charter bounds with a *weard-setl* recorded as one of the boundary marks between the two. The location is still known as Beacon Hill and, indeed, it is known to have served this function at the time of the Spanish Armada. The Yatesbury beacon considered above was most likely tied into the West Saxon system by reference to the beacon at Odstock, near to the burghal hidage fort and shire centre at Wilton, using one or two intermediate beacons. The Odstock beacon, recorded as *weardanhylle* in a charter of 928, was locked into a network looking northward from the Isle of Wight to *cwicelmeshlæw* in Berkshire (the shire meeting place) and north-eastward into Surrey (**33**). As Hill has noted, the landscape itself is probably the best guide to the location of major signalling stations. For the more local networks, however, a more detailed approach is required.

In an urban context, traces of the Late Anglo-Saxon civil defence of London are perhaps preserved in place-names such as Tilbury, Essex, which is sited on the north bank of the Thames Estuary opposite Dartford in Kent to the south. At Westminster, the name Tothill Street records the memory of a 'look-out hill'. Such sites very likely formed part of a signalling chain stretching from Shoebury, or 'protection burh', in Essex, where the Thames flows out into the North Sea, to London and beyond. *Burhs* with personal names such as Tilbury, or 'Tila's burh', probably record the names of individuals with military obligations who were responsible for their foundation or maintenance. The *Rectitudines Singularum Personarum* states that the thegn's duties include 'equipping a guard ship and guarding the coast' whereas the cottar might be called upon to keep 'watch on the sea-coast'

The settlement pattern along the course of the Thames to the west of London is suggestive of a planned exercise to maximise visibility either way along the river. Many of the known medieval settlements have Anglo-Saxon origins with places such as Brentford and Chelsea situated on river bends. Whilst this preference for location might seem purely logical on a number of grounds, an element of defensive concern is probable.

The visibility between and around individual settlements would have been substantially improved by the presence of towers which served a sighting and, perhaps, sounding, role. David Parsons has recently reviewed the evidence for specific type of Late Anglo-Saxon masonry towers called 'turriform naves'. Stone towers such as those at Earl's Barton, Northamptonshire (**colour plate 8**) and Jevington, Sussex seemingly represent the tower or burh-gate required by thegns in the *Geþyncðo*. Parsons suggests that the lower stages of such towers probably functioned as a private chapel, as indicated by the crosses carved on the heads of the ground floor windows and the stone roundel with a cross built into the south facing wall at ground level at Earl's Barton (**colour plate 9**). The first floor of the tower is interpreted as a part of a private residence entered via the narrow doorway visible in the south wall of the tower and presumably a timber structure lay to the south. There is documentary evidence for secular residential accommodation of this type in the form of a mid-eleventh century charter that notes how Wihtgar, son of Earl Ælfric, 'dwelt in a certain tower where the hospital now is' in either Bury St Edmunds or Clare in Suffolk. The upper storey at Earl's Barton represents a clear exhibition of the status of the owner, by its extravagant use of architectural detail strongly reminiscent of timber architecture (**colour plate 10**).

The tower at Earl's Barton is located adjacent to an earthwork of probable pre-conquest date (**colour plate 11**) and it is tempting to the see the tower sited within a fortified enclosure or *burh*. Furthermore, on the basis of the discussion above, it seems that the term burh-gate might account for a range of physical features from a free-standing tower with outer defences, to an earthen enclosure with a signalling beacon.

The judicial system

When groups of grisly burials are encountered, either by chance or from archaeological excavations, there is a tendency to ascribe the remains to battles or massacres. The heroic campaigns of conquest undertaken by the Early Anglo-Saxon kings eager to extend their territories and the ravaging of the Viking armies from the late eighth century are commonly held to account for unusual burials.

1 *The shire meeting-place for Berkshire at cwicelmeshlæw, on the Ridgeway near East Hendred (now in Oxfordshire). The Anglo-Saxon Chronicle under the year 1006 records how, after burning Wallingford, the Vikings 'turned along Ashdown to cwicelmeshlæw and waited there for what had been proudly threatened, for it had often been said that if they went to cwicelmeshlæw they would never get to the sea' – although they did, after beating the English in battle at Kennet and carting off their booty!* Sarah Semple

2 *The Oxna Mere or 'Pond of the Oxen' mentioned in the bounds of Stanton St Bernard, Wiltshire, dating to 957, sometimes known as 'England's oldest pond'. Dewponds were once a common feature of chalk downland areas and the Stanton example is a rare survival.* Author

3 *An ideal landscape for dividing into agricultural estates. This view of the northern scarp of the Pewsey Vale in north-east Wiltshire clearly explains the strip-like shape of estates in the area, which encompass the full variety of terrain.* Author

4 *A drove road running from the village of Stanton St Bernard, Wiltshire up onto the downs. This road was probably in existence by at least the Late Anglo-Saxon period, but the scars of long abandoned predecessors indicate that the position of routeways could be gradually changed by the seasonal avoidance of badly rutted stretches.* Author

5 *The East Wansdyke at the northern end of the Stanton St Bernard estate. Old English boundary descriptions of 957 and 960 record the site of a gallows sited upon the bank toward the end of the stretch shown in this photograph.* Author

6 *A sherd of Late Anglo-Saxon pottery from the base of the ditch surrounding the excavated beacon platform at Yatesbury, Wiltshire. Note the stamps around the shoulder of the vessel, probably made with a bone tool, and the indentations along the top of the rim. Scale 1cm divisions.* Mike Halliwell

7 *The prehistoric origins of Silbury Hill are well known, but the mound served as a fort in the Late Anglo-Saxon period guarding local routeways and providing an intermediate sighting point for a regional network of signalling beacons. The stepped appearance of the top of the mound marks the position of a timber revetment.* Author

8 *The thegnly tower at Earl's Barton, Northamptonshire. The ground floor served as a chapel, the first floor as part of a residential complex, whilst the top served to emphasise the status of its owner. The parapet is a later addition.* Author

9 *The cross motifs found above the ground floor windows at Earl's Barton on the south side, along with the cross-inscribed roundel. These features support an interpretation of the lowest stage of the tower as a chapel. The narrow doorway visible at first floor level suggests that this stage formed part of a residential complex extending further to the south.* Author

10 *The upper storey at Earl's Barton showing the extravagant use of architectural detail in the windows, but also the thin stone strips, known as pilasters, reminiscent of timber building techniques and styles.* Author

11 *The massive defensive ditch to the north of Earl's Barton church. It is unclear whether the ditch originally enclosed the church, but this seems likely. The Earl's Barton thegnly residence constitutes that of a wealthy individual.* Author

12 *Metal objects from a high-status site at Bawsey, Norfolk, probably the site of a monastery. The finds include so-called hooked-tags for fastening purses or garters, a strap-end of typical ninth-century type, a pin with a decorated head and a stylus or writing implement.* Norfolk Museums Service

13 *Excavations at Flixborough, Lincolnshire. Parts of buildings are represented by postholes cut into the subsoil.* © Humber Field Archaeology

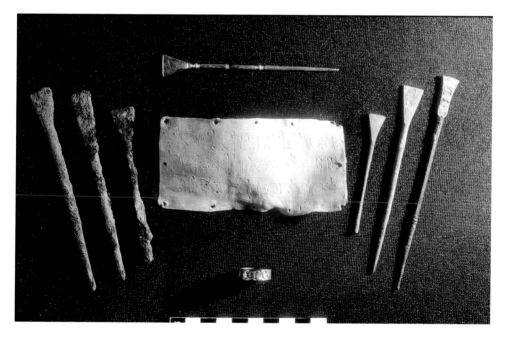

14 *Evidence for literacy from Flixborough. The inscribed lead plaque and ring indicate literate owners, but the styli provide indisputable evidence for the practice of writing at the site. Scale 1cm divisions.* © Humber Field Archaeology

15 *The hoard of iron tools from Flixborough, which includes draw-knives and spoon-bits in addition to a fine collection of axes. The equipment from the hoard is typical of the range of tools that would have been required on a day-to-day basis at a busy estate centre.*
© Humber Field Archaeology

16 *The two lead tanks that contained the hoard of iron tools from Flixborough. Scale 1cm divisions.*
© Humber Field Archaeology

17 *Excavations at Hamwic (Anglo-Saxon Southampton). This aerial view of part of the Six Dials area (Site SOU 169) shows the characteristic mass of postholes and pits indicating dense occupation.* © Cultural Services, Southampton City Council

18 *The Late Anglo-Saxon church at Alton Barnes, Wiltshire. The nave is Late Anglo-Saxon with characteristic pilaster-strips running up the walls, although now largely obscured by render. The doorway is original, having been partially blocked to form a window. The chancel is of the eighteenth century. Such churches would have been a common sight on rural estates by the late eleventh century.* Author

19 *A view down a timber lined well shaft at Six Dials (Site SOU 30). Scale 1m.* © Cultural Services, Southampton City Council

20 *A cross-section through the filling of a pit at Six Dials (SOU 169). Note the so-called tip-lines, which indicate that at least the lower half of the pit was filled from the left. Scale 2m.* © Cultural Services, Southampton City Council

21 *A selection of sceattas from Dunston in Norfolk.* Norfolk Museums Service

22 *Building A at Steyning, West Sussex, facing south after excavation. The building was originally formed of timber planks and posts set upright in the postholes shown. Scale 2m.* Mark Gardiner

23 *One of the carefully cut postholes at the southern end of Building A at Steyning. Although the timbers have rotted long ago, the shape of a radially-split plank is left for the archaeologist to record in the form of the packing stones around it. Scale 20cm.* Mark Gardiner

24 *An inscribed gold ring of ninth-century date from Steyning. The ring is inscribed 'Aescwulf owns me' in a manner found on other objects of the period. Scale 1cm divisions.* Mark Gardiner

25 *A view along the Anglo-Saxon highway between Ramsbury, seat of a bishop from 909, and theprobable Burghal Hidage fort at Chisbury to the south. Note the sunken appearance of the road.* Author

The dramatic written records of early England give an impression of a violent society accustomed to strife, banditry and lawlessness. Such accounts, however, are contained in sources such as the *Anglo-Saxon Chronicle*, which tend to neglect the more mundane aspects of life.

Once the larger kingdoms became more securely established from the late seventh and eighth centuries, the maintenance of peace and social stability required an enforceable and practical system of justice. The poetic and prose sources tell us about prisons at royal manors, open air judicial courts held every four weeks, the judicial ordeal overseen by the church and, finally, about the range of punishments meted out to those found guilty.

The law codes issued by English kings from the seventh to the eleventh century mention a range of capital offences and, from the tenth century, state that executed wrongdoers were not to be buried in consecrated ground. The administrative structure of later Anglo-Saxon England is well-documented and has been studied in depth by historians, geographers and archaeologists with the general conclusion that the Anglo-Saxon landscape became increasingly rigidly organised. By the close of the tenth century at the latest, prison, court, church and place of execution can be seen operating within each administrative district, termed the Hundred.

Imprisonment

Prior to judgement certain offenders are likely to have been placed in confinement, either for their own safety from those seeking retribution, or for the safety of the community if the offence was particularly heinous. Before the appearance of formal prisons or lock-ups on royal manors, confinement of wrongdoers was probably within the nearest secure structure. The laws of Wihtred, king of Kent (690–725), record that 'he who catches and secures him [a thief], shall have half his value.' The laws of Ine (688–726) describe the penalty for 'he who captures a thief or has a captured thief given into his custody, and allows him to escape, or suppresses knowledge of the theft, shall pay for the thief according to his wergeld.' It is probably significant that a sub-clause to the law previously cited reads 'If he is an ealdorman he shall forfeit his 'shire' unless the king is willing to pardon him.'. This statement suggests that prisons could be maintained on the estates of high-ranking persons although *ad hoc* use of certain other buildings/settlements undoubtedly continued.

From the late eighth century prisons were apparently maintained at the *cynges tun*, or royal manor, and are evidenced by royal charters and Old English Literature.

The earliest references to imply a prison on a royal estate come from two charters of Cenwulf of Mercia which state that 'if a malefactor is three times apprehended, he shall be handed over to the royal vill' The literary evidence for the physical appearance of early prisons is limited. A description in the Old English poem *Juliana*, probably written by the Mercian poet Cynewulf early in the late eighth or ninth century, relates how Juliana's oppressor 'instructed that she be taken to prison,' and that 'the prison door, the work of hammers, was fastened with a bar'. The Genesis B poem, speculatively dated to the mid-ninth century (from MS Junius 11 of *c.*1000), contains a description of hell which may contain some contemporary influence on the nature of a place of confinement. The relevant passage reads:

> But bonds of iron encircle me; a halter of chain yokes me. I am powerless, such hard hell fetters have fast laid hold of me... Fetters of links, a cruel chain, have impeded my movement, deprived me of my motion. My feet are shackled, my hands tethered. The ways are blocked through these hell-gates so that I cannot escape at all from these trammels. Great bars of tough iron forged in fire surround me and with them God has tethered me by the neck.

The clearest evidence for the use of prisons as a punishment, as opposed to pre-trial or pre-execution confinement, is contained in the laws of Alfred and reads:

> If, however, he pledges himself to something which it is lawful to carry out and proves false to his pledge, he shall humbly give his weapons and possessions to his friends to keep, and remain 40 days in prison at a royal manor, and undergo there whatever [sentence] the bishop prescribes for him; and his relatives shall feed him if he himself has no food.

Further significant references occur in Alfred's translation of Augustine's *Soliloquies*. In Book I it is stated that 'it is likewise with the estates of every king: some men are in the chamber, some in the hall, some on the threshing-floor, some in prison'. This suggests widespread prisons and is supported by a further comment in Book III that 'rather, the situation is the same for them as it is for the men who in this life are brought to a king's prison and who everyday may see their friends and ask of them what they wish'.

There is further evidence from the laws of Athelstan relating to confinement of thieves for 40 days, with sorcerers and witches receiving 120 days, and to imprisonment of formerly convicted thieves before going to judicial ordeal. Cnut's second law-code states that 'no condemned man shall ever be put to death during the Sunday festival...., but he shall be arrested and kept in custody until the festival is over.'

The possibility of adding to evidence for imprisonment by archaeological methods is slim as there is little indication from the pictorial record to indicate that restraints such as iron shackles were employed in the period. A recent survey of Iron Age and Roman finds of shackles included a consideration of post-Roman examples, with Winchester producing the only known finds of Anglo-Saxon date. Late tenth- to late eleventh-century levels at the Old Minster produced two pairs of shackles and one single example, whereas eleventh-century levels associated with Houses IX and X at Lower Brook Street produced a single find. The context of the Old Minster finds is difficult to explain, although those undergoing judicial ordeals would have visited the structure. Certainly, one would expect shackles to have been removed prior to ordeal, although the finds could be viewed as 'spares' kept on the premises. The Lower Brook Street example is from a domestic context and it is possible, given that only half a pair of shackles is represented, that the find is simply a piece of scrap.

Without artefactual evidence, the possibility of identifying prisons from structural remains is severely hampered. Two *possibilities* have been advanced. At the Anglo-Saxon 'palace' at Cheddar in Somerset, the excavator suggested that the amorphous collection of postholes (Building R) immediately to the west of the south end of the Period 1 Long Hall may have been a prison (see Chapter 4 for the Cheddar excavations). In the north of England, Professor Rosemary Cramp's excavations at the seventh-century Northumbrian monastery of Wearmouth, revealed a sunken room, in an angle between walls belonging to the later Anglo-Saxon or early Norman phases of development. Tentative interpretations proposed either an external strong room or a prison. Perhaps the masonry towers found at sites of *thegnly* status would have served on occasion as places of confinement, somewhat in the nature of the village lock-ups of the later medieval and post-medieval periods. Without more concrete evidence these possibilities can only ever remain such, although it is hoped that future excavations of high-status secular sites in particular will eventually provide indisputable examples.

In summary, from the latest Kentish laws of Wihtred, it seems to have been the prerogative of the person apprehending the accused to confine him/her although the motivation appears limited to the pre-trial stage of proceedings. From the reign of Ine there is evidence that, in Wessex, *ealdormen* might have the responsibility of maintaining prisons and by the end of the eighth century the Mercian evidence suggests prisons on royal estates, a picture which clearly emerges in the laws and other writings of Alfred in the late 800s. The earlier tenth century and the reign of Athelstan reveal the role of prisons in the judicial process in even more detail.

Judgement

The first mention of judicial hearings before an assembly comes from the laws of the Kentish kings Hlothere and Eadric. The relevant caption reads: 'If one man brings a charge against another, and if he meets the man, at an assembly or meeting, the latter shall always provide the former with a surety, and render him such satisfaction as the judges of Kent shall prescribe for them'. As noted earlier in this chapter, the composition of these early assemblies is unclear and the right to attend may have been restricted to the higher ranks.

In later Anglo-Saxon England lawsuits were heard at a public assembly, the hundred court, whose meetings were held at least from the time of Edward the Elder when '*ælc gerefa hæbbe gemot a ymbe feower wucan*' 'each reeve was to hold a meeting every four weeks'. The courts referred to in Edward's laws were not termed hundred courts, but Henry Loyn has argued convincingly for their becoming so, based on their identical functions. As noted previously, the hundred is first mentioned explicitly in the laws of Edgar in the statement known as the *Hundred Ordinance*. Shire and borough courts were to meet twice and three times a year respectively. Appeals from the hundred court could be taken to the shire court or to the king, although by the time of the issue of Cnut's laws access to the monarch seems to have been effectively restricted by the development of a ranked system of appeal.

The charters and other evidence cited above indicate that the concept of public assembly was current before the reign of Alfred and probably became formally established during the period of micro-kingdoms and early state formation.

34 *A reconstruction of a judicial hearing before a hundred court. Royal and ecclesiastical officials oversee the proceedings from the top of the meeting mound.* Drawn by Sarah Semple

It is only in the later documents that the precise judicial functions of assemblies are defined. Æthelred, in his Wantage law code issued in 997, set out provisions for the establishment of peace in the *wapentakes* of the Danish Five Boroughs. Amongst these, provision was made for 12 leading *thegns,* accompanied by the king's *reeve,* to swear upon relics that [during a hearing] they would accuse no innocent man nor conceal any guilty one. This evidence has been taken as the earliest reference to a jury of presentment, which, incidentally, was also expected to produce a unanimous verdict.

At the beginning of a lawsuit the plaintiff summoned the defendant to appear before the hundred court, which was presided over by the king's *reeve* (**34**). If the defendant failed to come to answer the case against him on a number of occasions he lost the case by default. Furthermore, if the fines were not paid, or the offence was capital and the offender had absconded, he became an outlaw.

Where the defendant appeared, it was common practice for the plaintiff to take an oath swearing to the honesty of his motives followed by the defendant swearing to prove his innocence. The defendant swore with the aid of oath-helpers, for the acquisition of which time was allowed to the defendant, and the value of the oath was linked to social rank. If the defendant and his oath-helpers presented a satisfactory case, the suit ended and the defendant was cleared. If, however, the defendant was either a suspicious character, had committed previous offences, or was caught in the act, he was no longer oath-worthy. In such cases the plaintiff and his compurgators had the right to swear to the defendant's guilt. When the plaintiff was successful, then the defendant was subject to judicial ordeal.

Ordeal

The first reference to judicial ordeal is contained in the laws of Ine concerning theft, although the *Lex Salica* (the laws of the Salian Franks) shows that the hot ordeal was employed from the early sixth century on the continent. An early reference to the hot water ordeal comes from seventh-century Ireland where there are a number of references of the seventh/eighth and ninth century, but the English version is apparently the result of Frankish influence.

Amongst the more widely discussed liturgical apparatus belonging to a superior church, such as relics, vestments and books, equipment relating to the judicial ordeal should be expected. The process and material requirements of ordeal are clearly set out in two documents; the laws of Athelstan and a text entitled the *Decree concerning Hot Iron and Water*. Both warrant quotation in full. The former reads:

> 23. If anyone engages to undergo an ordeal, he shall come three days before to the mass-priest who is to consecrate it, and he shall feed himself on bread and water and salt and herbs before he proceeds thither, and he shall attend mass on each of the three days. And on the day he has to go to the ordeal, he shall make an offering and attend communion; and then before he goes to the ordeal, he shall swear an oath that according to the public law he is innocent of the accusation.

> 23.1 And if the ordeal is by water he shall sink to a depth of one-and-a-half ells on the rope. If the ordeal is by [hot] iron three days shall elapsebefore the hand is unwrapped.

> 23.2 And every man shall precede his accusation with an oath, as we have already declared, and everyone who is present in both parties shall fast according to the command of God and the archbishop. And there shall not be more than twelve on either side. If, however, the accused man is one of a party greater than twelve, the ordeal shall be invalidated, unless they will leave him.

The 'Decree' runs as follows:

> 1. And with regard to the ordeal, by the commands of God and the archbishop and all the bishops, we enjoin that no-one shall enter the church after the fire with which the iron or water for the ordeal is to be heated has been brought in, except the mass-priest and him who has to go to trial. And from the stake to the mark, nine feet shall be measured by the feet of him who goes to the trial.

1.1 And if the trial is by water, it shall be heated until it becomes so hot as to boil, whether the vessel (containing it) be made of iron or brass, lead or clay.

1.2 And if the accusation is 'single', the hand shall be plunged in up to the wrist in order to reach the stone; if it is 'threefold', up to the elbow.

1.3 And when the ordeal is ready two men shall go in from either party, and they shall be agreed that it is as hot as we have declared.

1.4 And [then] an equal number of men from each party shall enter, and stand along the church on both sides of the ordeal, and all these shall be fasting and shall have abstained from their wives during the night; and the mass-priest shall sprinkle holy water over them all, and each of them shall taste the holy water. And [the mass-priest] shall give them all the book and the symbol of Christ's cross to kiss. And no-one shall continue to make up the fire after the consecration has begun, but the iron shall lie upon the embers until the last collect. Then it shall be laid upon the post, and no other words shall be spoken in the church, except that God be earnestly prayed to make clear the whole truth.

1.5 And the accused shall go to the ordeal, and his hand shall be sealed up; and after three days it shall be inspected [in order] to ascertain whether it has become discoloured or remained clean within the sealed wrappings.

1.6 And if anyone breaks these rules, the ordeal shall in his case be invalidated, and he shall pay a fine of 120 shillings to the king.

The judicial ordeal is the guilt-absolving element of the Christian period judicial system. The ritual is likely to have been conducted in superior churches and a law of Aethelred states that 'every ordeal shall take place in a royal manor'. This situation almost certainly reflects the close association of minster churches with royal manors. The ordeal ceased to play a part in the judicial process, due to declining faith in its effectiveness, during the twelfth century and, in 1215, the Fourth Lateran Council declared that the clergy were no longer to conduct proceedings.

The use of wells or cisterns for cold water ordeal is very likely, although the possibilities of finding tangible archaeological confirmation are extremely small. The nature of the apparatus of the cold water ordeal is described in a Carolingian text, which describes a substantial tank, but the text also notes how the individual undergoing the ordeal was bound in a crouching position prior to immersion. Theoretically a bound person tied to a rope could be lowered into a wide variety of water holding features. Archaeological and topographical information about the layout at certain principal church sites has provided examples of churches located adjacent to substantial wells, cisterns and ponds. Examples include Bath, Wells, Barton-on-Humber, Winchester, Glastonbury and Lincoln.

Punishment

A range of punishments is described in the documentary record and the following paragraphs outline the nature of offences and atonements. Fines always formed the predominant means of punishment and the earliest references to capital punishment occur in the laws of Ine. These concern fighting in the king's house, travelling unannounced and the fate of absconding slaves, who were to be hanged. Elsewhere in the code, removal of the hand or foot was prescribed for common theft. In the near contemporary laws of Wihtred, freemen and slaves caught stealing could expect to lose their lives and those travelling unannounced could meet the same end. Capital offences in Alfred's laws are plotting against the life of either the king or one's lord and fighting in the king's hall. Stealing from the church resulted in the loss of the hand that committed the theft. The laws of Edward the Elder and Guthrum state how wizards and sorcerers should be utterly destroyed.

The laws of Athelstan see a marked increase in the range of capital offences and give more detail of the punishments. Anyone seized in the act of stealing over the age of 12 was to lose their life. A thief who defended himself, or fled, was subject to the death penalty, as were others declared outlaws. Moneyers issuing base or light coins could have the hand which committed the crime cut off and fastened upon the mint whilst individuals swearing false oath were denied burial in consecrated ground. Athelstan's fourth code is concerned largely with theft and prescribes the various forms of death penalty for thieves. Death could be expected by thieves taking flight and by those who might harbour them; free women might be thrown from a cliff or drowned (that the latter penalty could be incurred for witchcraft by the reign of Edgar is demonstrated by a charter of Bishop Æthelwold which records the drowning of a woman at (a) London Bridge between 963–75); male slaves could be stoned and females burnt. Athelstan's fifth and sixth codes largely reiterate earlier legislation although the minimum age for the death penalty was raised from 12 to 15.

Edmund's (939–46) first set of laws was concerned with ecclesiastical regulation and burial in consecrated ground was forbidden to those who failed to observe celibacy or who had intercourse with a nun. Furthermore, the latter clause prescribes the same for murderers and adulterers. Edmund's second code mentions violation of the king's protection and attacks on a man's house as capital crimes and his third code provides the first mention of mutilation in relation to gangs of thieving slaves whose leader was to be hanged.

Edgar's laws prescribe capital punishment for both treason against a lord and non-payment of rent and decapitation for swearing falsely that livestock was bought in the presence of witnesses.

The substantial legislation of Æthelred gives further examples of offences that preclude burial in consecrated ground, such as lack of surety, violent burglary and the murder of innocent persons on the king's highway. Decapitation could result from a second trial by judicial ordeal or breach of the peace inside a town. Other capital crimes were striking false coins and minting 'in woods', deserting an army under personal command of the king, remaining near the king if excommunicated and plotting against the king's life.

The latest laws to be issued in the period were those of Cnut. The death penalty could be applied to corrupt reeves, those violating the protection of the church and the king, for sorcery, theft and treason against one's lord, for being untrustworthy, maintaining an excommunicated man or an outlaw and for deserting one's lord or comrades whilst on an expedition. Punishment for issuing base or light coins remained the removal of a hand and punishments for the untrustworthy were extended to removal of the hands and feet. Mutilation increased considerably as a favoured means of punishment, which has been explained in terms of Archbishop Wulfstan's overriding influence in the making of law.

Failure to acquire the 'true belief', or to be found untrustworthy with no surety, could entail the forfeiture of burial in consecrated ground.

Specific locations where capital punishments were carried out were present from the earliest period of Christianised judicial authority. The epic poem *Beowulf* mentions gallows on two occasions. Lines 2444–46 use an execution scene to conjure an emotion 'grief such as this a grey-headed man might feel if he saw his son in youth riding the gallows'. whereas lines 2940–42 see the threat of hanging made to enemies in war; 'he promised horrors to that unhappy band, saying that on the morrow he would mutilate them with the edges of the sword, and string some up on the gallows as sport for the birds'. The eighth-century Ruthwell Cross runic inscription mentions gallows, but with reference directly to the crucifixion itself, whereas the mid-ninth century (or later) poem *The Dream of the Rood* which partly follows the Ruthwell inscription, records how: 'Strong enemies seized me [the Rood] there, fashioned me as a spectacle for themselves and required me to hoist up their felons. There men carried me upon their shoulders until they set me up on a hill ' (ibid., 159–61). In the late eighth- or early ninth-century work *Juliana*, the saint is led 'close to the border of the country' for her execution.

These literary references, although not proving a developed legal system in the eighth and ninth centuries, do suggest familiarity with the instruments of formal judicial killing and give insights into locational characteristics. Several later poems include references to execution. *The Fortunes of Men*, from the later tenth century Exeter Book, contains the following passage:

> One shall ride the high gallows and upon his death hang until his soul's treasury, his bloody bone-framed body, disintegrates. There the raven black of plumage will pluck out the sight from his head and shred the soulless corpse — and he cannot fend off with his hands the loathsome bird of prey from its evil intent. His life is fled and, deprived of his senses, beyond hope of survival, he suffers his lot, pallid upon the beam, enveloped in the mist of death. His name is damned.

A further Old English text, *Maxims II,* metaphorically describes the fate of a wrongdoer in the line 'The thief must go forth in murky weather' and also in no uncertain terms when it is later stated that 'the criminal must hang and fairly pay the recompense because he previously committed a crime against mankind.'

Execution sites

With an outline of English judicial arrangements in the localities to work from, the potential for an archaeological dimension becomes apparent — if capital offenders were executed at specific locations and precluded burial in consecrated ground, then execution cemeteries must have been widespread in later Anglo-Saxon England. Archaeology provides important evidence for the existence of an organised system of execution sites located on the boundaries between individual hundreds, presumably because the burden of management fell between the two. About 20 cemeteries are known which fit the criteria of judicial execution sites. These are found in southern and eastern England, from Malling Hill, near Lewes in Sussex to Walkington Wold in the East Riding of Yorkshire. The common features of execution cemeteries fall into two groups; the characteristics of the burials; and, landscape associations, such as prominent siting, re-use of prehistoric barrows or linear earthworks of various date, and proximity to boundaries.

In recent years osteologists have begun to consider in detail the pathological traces that hand-to-hand combat might leave on the human skeleton. Research suggests various blows to the upper body particularly the arms and the head. Decapitations from Anglo-Saxon execution cemeteries, however, are characterised by untidy, and in many cases excessively violent, beheading from behind probably with a sword. Blows to the back of the neck could extend from the shoulder blades to the top of the head. A fear of the corpse rising from the dead has been offered to explain the practice of decapitation. Particular fear appears to have surrounded the man from the Roche Court Down cemetery in Wiltshire whose head had been smashed and buried separately from the body within a ring of flints. Evidence for the public display of heads comes in the form of weather-worn skulls buried without the lower jaw, which had presumably dropped off, and from Anglo-Saxon boundary descriptions which refer to *heafod stoccan* (head stakes) as marks. At Stockbridge Down in Hampshire one of the 43 shallow graves there was found to contain the burial of a decapitated man accompanied by a similarly treated dog (**35**). Accounts from medieval Europe mention the prosecution of an extraordinary variety of animals, including flies, field mice and eels, but the Stockbridge man and dog were probably executed on a charge of bestiality, with man reduced to the ideological status of beast in terms of the mode of execution and burial.

Execution burials are also found face down and include the adult male from Meon Hill, Hampshire buried with a large boulder on his back and inhumations from Guildown, Surrey, where one man's feet had been cut off at the knees, whilst another lay in a deep grave with his hands tied behind his back (**36**). A superstitious motive seems likely with the prone burials especially as they are often the deepest graves at execution sites. In a few instances bodies are found bent over backwards and it seems likely that such individuals were put to death whilst kneeling in their graves.

The most common mode of execution, however, was hanging. There is evidence for two-post gallows structures from execution sites at Sutton Hoo, Suffolk and South Acre, Norfolk among others, but the majority of evidence is provided by the large number of corpses found with the hands tied behind the back. In certain instances flexion of the hands has been noted and interpreted by Tony Waldron as an indicator of a violent death.

35 *The burial of a decapitated man and dog from the execution cemetery at Stockbridge Down, Hampshire.* Taken from Hill 1937

36 *A man buried prone with the hands tied behind the back from the execution cemetery at Guildown, Surrey.* Taken from Lowther 1931

37 *A reconstruction of an Anglo-Saxon execution site. Three men hang from a gallows sited upon a linear earthwork with extensive landscape views.* Drawn by Sarah Semple

Execution victims were commonly buried in twos and threes, indicating that such individuals were executed, or at least displayed hanging from a gallows together. In general, however, little care was taken with the burials of wrongdoers with no apparent concern for grave orientation and the minimum of effort invested in the digging of the graves (with the exception of the 'superstitious' burials).

Two thirds of the excavated execution sites are associated with barrows of prehistoric or Anglo-Saxon origin, whereas the remainder of sites is located upon linear earthworks. In general the sites afford commanding views frequently within sight of important routes of communication by water and road (**37**). All of the excavated sites lay on boundaries; about a third lie on county boundaries, and all but two lie upon hundred boundaries. Such strong locational tendencies suggest that the choice of both earthworks and principal boundaries was common practice in the later Anglo-Saxon period.

Armed with the knowledge that the excavated sites lay upon boundaries, the descriptions of the limits of Anglo-Saxon estates prove a fruitful source for contemporary terminology and give further confirmation that execution cemeteries were located upon hundred boundaries. The results of research by the author have shown that 87% of execution sites mentioned in charter bounds lie on the boundaries of hundreds. The bounds of Rolleston in Staffordshire of 1008 refer to '*ðan þorne þer ða þeofes licgan*', or 'the

38 *Execution sites and hundred boundaries in Hampshire.* Redrawn from Reynolds 1998

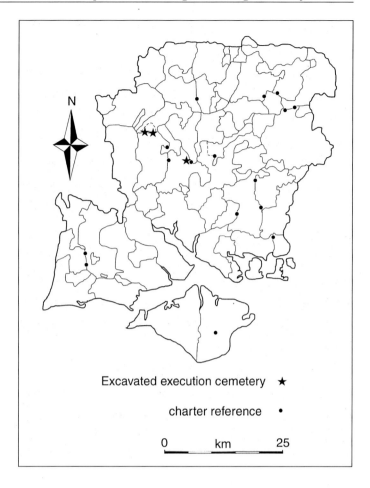

Excavated execution cemetery ★

charter reference •

0   km   25

thorn where the thieves lie', those of Stanton St Bernard, Wiltshire of 957 and 960 mention the *wearhroda*, or felons cross, atop the great linear earthwork of east Wansdyke. Other terms include *heaðenan byrgels* (heathen burials) and *cwealmstow* (killing place). The great majority of the places of execution and burial recorded in boundary clauses share characteristics with the excavated sites including elevated location and inter-visibility with routeways.

The choice of the hundred boundaries as a fitting repository for executed offenders probably reflects the desire to banish social outcasts to the geographical limits of local territories. In Hampshire, for example, 100% of sites can be shown to lie on the boundaries of the Domesday Hundreds (**38**), whilst other counties produce similar results. The choice of elevated locations suggests a further visual motivation, as those travelling by execution sites would have looked up to see corpses hanging effectively between heaven and earth being deemed unworthy of both. The reuse of prehistoric features is of interest and the topic has attracted much recent attention. The choice of such sites as suitable burial places for outcasts seemingly reflects Germanic lore. Associations between barrows and dragons are well known in epic poetry such as *Beowulf*. Barrows were widely perceived as the houses of dragons and demons and it appears that, in addition to exclusion from consecrated ground, offenders were interred in places where they would endure eternal torment from supernatural monsters. A Biblical motivation for a number of aspects of Anglo-Saxon kingship has long been accepted and an analysis of the machinery of the judicial system suggests strong influence here also. The lengths of prison sentences prescribed in the laws of King Alfred and his successors are, in Biblical fashion, 40 and 120 days.

In summary, the study of execution cemeteries provides yet another indication of the potential of archaeology to address and broaden our knowledge of governance in later Anglo-Saxon England. The execution sites themselves serve only to underline the efficiency of the administration of systems of social control by the later Anglo-Saxon kings.

Now that people and landscape have been accounted for in terms of social organisation, the law and military organisation, we shall move on to consider the living conditions and workings of the countryside, where the majority of Anglo-Saxons lived out their daily experience.

4 The landscape: settlements in the countryside

Introduction

Any consideration of rural life before the Domesday Survey of 1086 relies increasingly upon the evidence from archaeological excavations as the principal source the further back in time one wishes to look. The great proliferation of land charters of tenth-century and later date are a major source for the Late Anglo-Saxon period, but for the eighth and ninth centuries archaeology is of prime importance. Social and economic historians concerned with matters of terminology, taxation and social hierarchies have largely dominated the study of the Anglo-Saxon rural peasantry. The contribution of archaeology has been to broaden the study to examine the nature of housing, diet, production and consumption, and social structure on a subtler basis. As Chapter 2 has shown, Anglo-Saxon society during the period 700–1100 was a stratified one. Over the period under consideration there were changes in terminology and the roles undertaken by particular individuals or classes of people. Archaeology provides data from which a detailed assessment of the reality of rural life can be attempted, and this chapter draws upon a series of excavated sites to explore the physical dimension of social stratification.

Generalisations can be made about the nature of settlement patterns in England throughout the period from 700–1100. In the uplands of south-western and northern England, dispersed farms appear to have been the norm, whereas certain of the sites considered below illustrate the existence of more organised groupings of farmsteads, or nucleated settlements, over a wide geographical area. The long-running academic study of nucleated-type villages has only recently begun to consider the full complexity of the settlement of the English landscape and it is now appreciated that there was considerable geographical variation in settlement type with a tier of dispersed settlements often concealed within so-called nucleated landscapes. This chapter begins with a consideration of the evidence for the upper strata of Anglo-Saxon society and then moves on to consider village and manorial origins by looking at both *thegnly* residences as well as those of peasant status involved in both communal and pastoral farming activities.

Kingly and *thegnly* settlements

There is all too little archaeological evidence from which the lifestyle of the English Kings can be reconstructed, but happily sufficiently more for a reasonably clear picture of the *thegnly* classes to be visualised. Professor Philip Rahtz's excavations at Cheddar, Somerset in the 1970s have provided the paradigm for royal settlement in England, although the Cheddar site and the later discovery of a purported 'palace' at Northampton have been subjected to rigorous debate and reinterpretation in recent years. The successive timber and stone halls of Middle Anglo-Saxon date excavated at Northampton are now seen as monastic buildings, as the site lies immediately to the east, and in axial alignment with, St Peter's minster church.

The impetus for re-thinking the nature of high-status settlements was provided by the problems of interpretation raised by the discovery in the 1980s of new sites yielding high-status finds at Flixborough, Lincolnshire and Brandon and Bawsey in Norfolk (**colour plate 12**). Until these discoveries were made, archaeologists had relied upon the characterisation of high-status finds assemblages from historically documented Anglo-Saxon monasteries to provide a benchmark to distinguish religious communities from secular ones. The root of the problem lies in making a distinction on purely archaeological grounds between monastic and secular estate centres. To further complicate matters, it seems that during the Middle Anglo-Saxon period there was little uniformity in the layout of monasteries.

The major excavated seventh-century monasteries at Jarrow and Wearmouth in Northumbria show close comparisons, but the sites together constituted a 'double monastery' founded by the same individual, a certain Benedict Biscop. Although linear arrangements of structures can be observed as a common characteristic of high-status Anglo-Saxon secular settlements, they are found also on monastic sites. There are good grounds, however, for assigning a monastic interpretation to sites where window glass is found and where there is evidence for concrete *'opus signinum'* floors in imitative Roman style.

Cemeteries are of course found at monastic sites, but also at secular ones. Burial data is capable of providing information about sex ratios and a heavy weighting toward either males or females, or a sexually exclusive population, would support a monastic interpretation rather than a more domestic one where one should expect mixed family groups.

A further difficulty is posed by the evidence for literacy recovered from certain sites in the form of *styli*, or writing implements. Whilst the art of literacy is likely to have been largely confined to monasteries, the increasing use of documentary administration with regard to rural affairs makes it equally likely that the larger secular estate centres would have had a resident cleric responsible for sending and receiving documents. It is well known that legislation was produced and charters attested at meetings of the king and his councillors. Such meetings, or *witans*, were often held at royal estate centres and provide a possible context for the finding of *styli* at such sites.

A further illustration of developments in archaeological interpretation is provided by Christopher Loveluck's work on the Flixborough settlement where he has emphasised

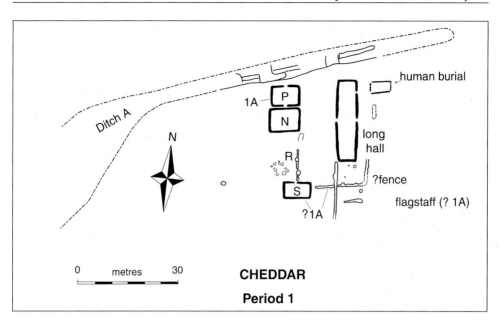

39 *The ninth-century royal residence at Cheddar, Somerset (Period 1).* Redrawn from Rahtz 1979

that the function of such sites is likely to change over time. Such a view allows not only for the finding of high-status artefacts on both religious and secular sites, but also for a particular site to become monastic in character and then revert to secular use or *vice versa*. Ultimately, we must use the available evidence and attempt to interpret it within the scope of what we already know about the period, and it is too easy to become preoccupied with problems rather than to postulate solutions.

Our view of ninth- to eleventh-century royal accommodation is derived exclusively from the Cheddar excavations. The site itself lies at the opening to the famous Gorge, and an Anglo-Saxon royal presence is confirmed by documentary evidence. The estate of Cheddar is mentioned in the will of King Alfred and, although a royal residence is not explicitly mentioned, it seems likely that the earliest phases of occupation relate to a royal holding.

The *witan* met three times at Cheddar during the tenth century, in 941, 956 and 968 under the patronage of kings Edmund, Eadwig and Edgar, respectively. Furthermore, a small number of land charters are known to have been attested at Cheddar and it has been suggested that of the large number of charters issued during King Eadwig's reign, a proportion of those issued in 956 may have been drawn up there. Cheddar's royal associations run on into the period following the Norman Conquest and the site is known to have been visited by Henry I and II.

The earliest period at Cheddar is dated to before *c*.930 and comprised a group of five timber buildings set to the south of a substantial drainage, or storm-water, ditch (**39**). The earliest coin from the site, a penny of King Alfred's father King Æthelwulf dated to *c*.845, suggests the origins of the settlement lie in the mid-ninth century, although an

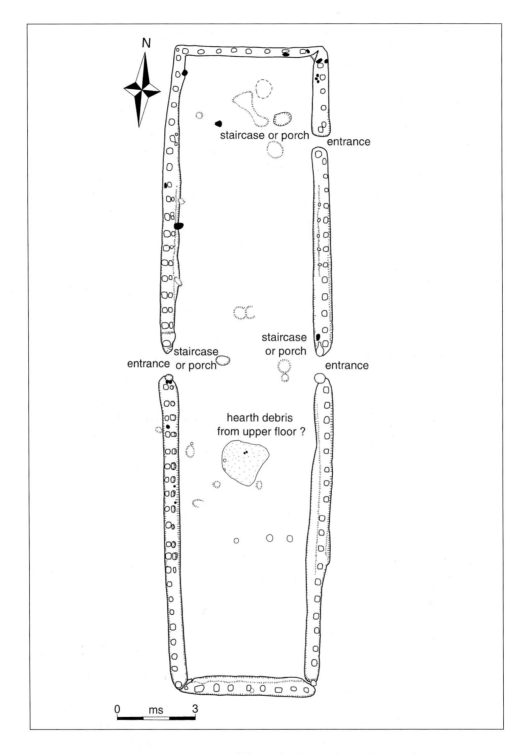

N

staircase or porch

entrance

staircase entrance or porch

staircase or porch

entrance

hearth debris from upper floor ?

0   ms   3

40 *The ninth-century (Period 1) Long Hall from Cheddar.* Redrawn from Rahtz 1979

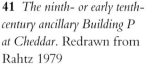

41 *The ninth- or early tenth-century ancillary Building P at Cheddar.* Redrawn from Rahtz 1979

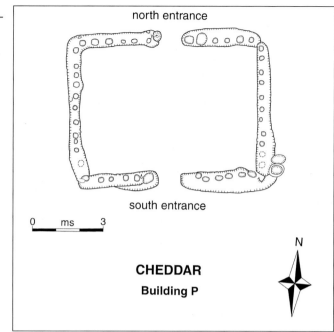

even earlier date is possible. The principal building of the first phase was a long hall, possibly of two storeys. The structure measured 24m in length, 5.5m wide at either end and just over 6m in the middle, thus describing a bow-sided building (**40**). The structure was aligned north-south and constructed using closely set squared timbers within a continuous foundation trench. The hall was entered via opposing doorways placed midway along the long walls, with a further opening on the eastside at the north end, possibly a service entrance. Paired posts along the inner face of part of the north wall led the excavator to postulate a second storey to the building. The presence of a hearth in the southern end of the hall is likely, although the surviving evidence did not permit a more precise interpretation. It is thought possible that the burnt material found within the long hall was derived from a collapsed upper floor hearth, although a former suspended floor at ground level would also account for the disturbed nature of the burnt clay and charcoal deposit.

The remaining four buildings probably served a range of functions associated with an estate centre, including private residential buildings and offices. Building N lay to the west of the long hall and was succeeded by Building P immediately to the north (**41**). Building S lay to the south-west of the long hall and appeared to relate to fence-lines both to the north and to the east, with the latter possibly forming part of an enclosure around the long hall. This arrangement of buildings outlines a courtyard-like area to the west of the long hall. A further structure, Building Z, lay to the east of the north end of the long hall and was lightly constructed of posts set or driven into individual holes, each some 0.4m apart. Close to the east end of Structure Z was an isolated human burial, seemingly with the hands tied behind the back. Perhaps the burial is that of a person executed under the auspices of a royal reeve and buried in unconsecrated ground. Isolated finds of unusual

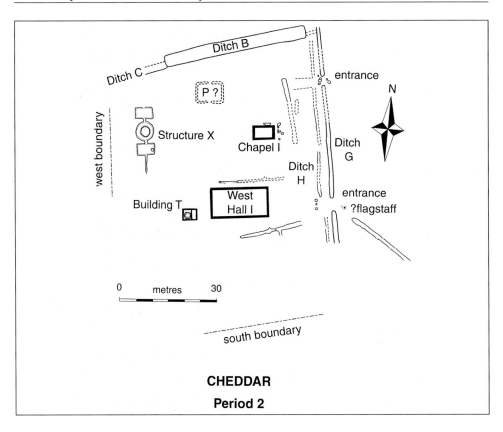

42 *The early tenth-century royal residence at Cheddar (Period 2).* Redrawn from Rahtz 1979

burials are known from a series of Anglo-Saxon settlements, such as Yarnton, Oxfordshire, Cottam, Humberside and the City of London, and these appear to represent the burials of outcasts prior to the widespread establishment of formal execution cemeteries from the tenth century.

During the late ninth and earlier tenth century the storm-water ditch to the north of the complex silted up. The relative occurrence of coins of *c.*845, *c.*870 and *c.*930 in the ditch fills, broadly date this process. The succeeding late tenth- or early eleventh-century phase of occupation, Period 2, saw a complete refurbishment of the site, possibly with the retention of Building P from Period 1 (**42**). A new hall was built on an east-west alignment in the southern part of the site whilst a masonry chapel was built on the site of the Period 1 long hall. The new hall was a substantial construction, measuring 17m in length and 9.1m in width, comprising 0.3m to 0.6m posts set 2.3m apart within substantial post-pits. In contrast to the more usual arrangement of opposed doorways midway along the long walls, the new hall was entered via openings at either end with a latrine, Building T, sited a few metres outside the west entrance.

A chapel was built using limestone rubble, and furnished with moulded windows and doorways, and faced with a heavy stucco painted with pseudo-ashlar decoration in

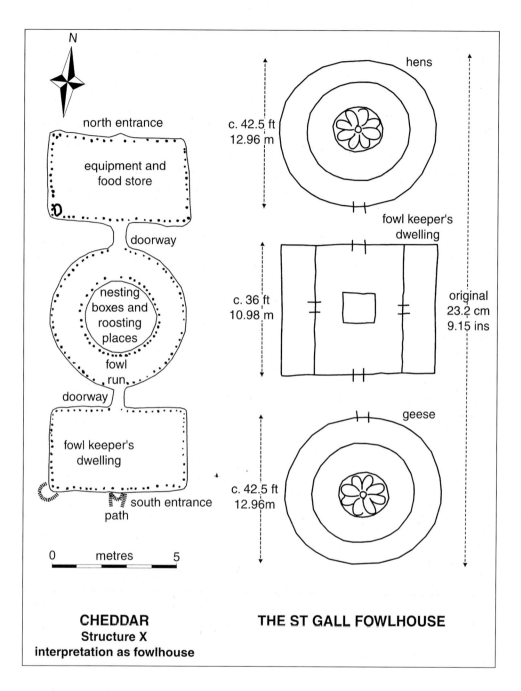

N

north entrance

equipment and
food store

doorway

nesting
boxes and
roosting
places

fowl
run

doorway

fowl keeper's
dwelling

south entrance
path

0   metres   5

CHEDDAR
Structure X
interpretation as fowlhouse

hens

c. 42.5 ft
12.96 m

fowl keeper's
dwelling

c. 36 ft
10.98 m

original
23.2 cm
9.15 ins

geese

c. 42.5 ft
12.96m

THE ST GALL FOWLHOUSE

43 *The possible fowl-house from Cheddar compared to a ninth-century sketch of a fowl-house from the monastery of St Gall, Switzerland.* Redrawn from Rahtz 1979

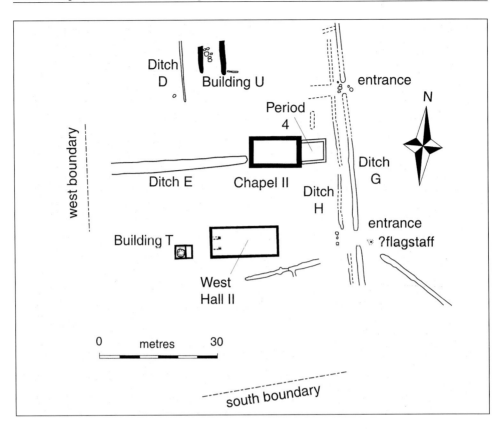

44 *The late tenth-century royal residence at Cheddar (Period 3).* Redrawn from Rahtz 1979

imitation of cut ashlar blocks. Interpretation of the building as a chapel rests on it being enclosed within the later chapels built at the site, although pseudo-ashlar is unknown in any other context at this date.

At the western edge of the site a remarkable structure formed of two rectangular parts on either side of a circular construction was found. The floor of the building was scooped some 0.3m into the ground, leaving a raised platform within the circular area, with the superstructure formed around closely spaced stakes. All three elements appear to have been joined as one, and the building lay on a north-south alignment. By comparison with the idealised ninth-century plan of the Swiss monastery at St Gall, it is suggested that the structure served as a fowl-house, with the north part serving as a store, the central element as the fowl-house itself and the south part serving as a dwelling for the fowl keeper (**43**). Further economic activity is indicated by the finding of fragmentary structures to the east of the chapel associated with evidence for smelting and iron forging. Substantial traces of small-scale metal casting and melting in gold and silver and evidence for enamel suggests jewellery manufacture as well as heavier goods.

Additional significant developments on the eastern side of the site included the construction of a ditched boundary with two entrances, the southernmost of which was formed of three posts and lay directly in line with the eastern doorway of the main hall. A massive posthole some 1m in both diameter and depth lay immediately outside the main gateway, and its filling contained a sherd of pottery suggesting it was filled at the end of Period 1 or during Period 2. Traces of stone packing survived which surrounded a void left by the rotted post that measured some 0.5m in diameter. Such a deeply-set isolated post is unusual and it is thought that a flagstaff or decorated pillar may have stood there.

Period 3 is dated to before the Norman Conquest and represents the last Anglo-Saxon modification of the site (**44**). The main hall was reduced in width to 7.6m, possibly reusing the timbers from the previous phase. The chapel was rebuilt on a grander scale, whilst the latrine building and the eastern boundary features were retained from Period 2. A ditch leading westward from the south-west corner of the new chapel indicates a reorganisation of the layout of the interior of the site, of which only the southern half was now occupied by the royal buildings. Structures to the north of this boundary presumably served the royal complex and these perhaps represent the accommodation of servants or other estate workers. It may be significant here that the fowl-house was made redundant by the new arrangements and it was perhaps relocated further to the north. Building U lay in the northern area to the east but parallel with an insubstantial north-south boundary. The structure was poorly built with stone rubble foundations on two sides and some evidence for associated light post settings, perhaps part of a lean-to attached to the main building. An industrial function is clearly borne out by iron working residues indicative of forging found within the building. Further waste products found within Structure U suggest the presence of iron furnaces in close proximity.

The objects from Cheddar are rather impressive in terms of range, but there are no spectacular finds such as those from Flixborough (see below). The metal finds included a range of dress fittings with some fine decorated ninth-century objects such as strap-ends (**45**). Only a handful of sherds of pottery were found relating to Period 1 and only few to Period 2. During Period 3 the range and quantity of vessels broadened to include lamps as well as a wider variety of cooking pots and dishes. The economy as indicted by the faunal remains suggests a reliance largely on cattle. Large dumps of animal bones were recovered from the ninth- and tenth-century infilling of the Period 1 northern boundary ditch and these appear to represent the remains of animals slaughtered at a prime stage of development. The absence of deer is of interest given the association of hunting with a royal presence in the area as attested by the story of King Edmund's narrow escape from death whilst involved in the chase in the vicinity of the Gorge. The range of agricultural and woodworking tools in the Cheddar assemblage accords well with the documentary evidence for tools and equipment at a major estate centre. Finds of Anglo-Saxon date include shears, a strike-a-light, tweezers and a chisel.

The complex at Cheddar is considered to have been a royal establishment from the outset, although the nature of occupation during Period 1 is more consistent with continuous occupation, perhaps by a royal reeve or a member of the royal family rather than by the King himself. Period 2 does not display this kind of activity and Philip Rahtz suggests that the site was occupied only periodically during the tenth and eleventh centuries on the occasion of significant royal assemblies.

The Flixborough excavations (**colour plate 13**) revealed a long-lived settlement of a

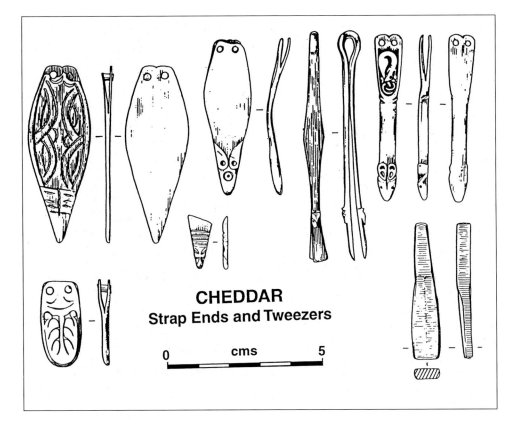

45 *Small finds from Cheddar including strap ends and tweezers.* Redrawn from Rahtz 1979

status befitting that of a wealthy estate centre for much of its existence. Occupation runs from the seventh century through to the late tenth or early eleventh century and the sequence is rather longer than usually found at Anglo-Saxon rural settlements. In common with other sites, the excavation only uncovered part of the settlement, but the dynamics of the Flixborough site are clearly complex. The site of a deserted medieval village lies 200m to the east of the excavated area, but the location of the parish church dedicated to All Saint's between the two suggests that all three may represent part of effectively the same settlement. It could be argued that the process known as settlement shift has occurred and a comparison drawn with the Early Anglo-Saxon site at Mucking considered in Chapter 1.

Post-excavation analyses of the results from the excavations at Flixborough are still in progress and it would be unwise to attempt a detailed period-by-period account of the site before they have been completed. Instead, some idea of the general character of the site will be given with reference to the impressive range of buildings and artefacts recovered.

The excavated site lies on a sand spur with a view over the floodplain of the River Trent to the west. Long-lived building plots were recorded with a total of at least 30 buildings in evidence. A remarkable feature of the site is the fact that stratified layers of occupation

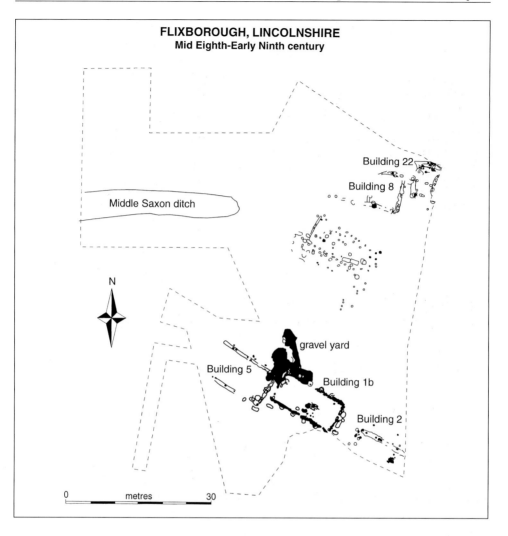

46 *Mid-eighth to early ninth-century occupation at Flixborough, Lincolnshire. Note the linear arrangement of buildings.* © Humber Field Archaeology

were found, in some cases separated from each other by dumps of domestic waste and demolition deposits. Large quantities of well-preserved animal bone was recovered from rubbish dumps, or middens.

Although at a preliminary stage, post-excavation analysis has allowed a simplified sequence of the development of the site to be assembled. The earliest features belong to the seventh century and include at least one rectangular timber structure, Building 5. Only the south-east end of Building 5 survived, but sufficient remained to establish the nature of its foundations; a continuous trench with a stone post-pad at one corner. The number and diversity of structures steadily increased until sometime during the first half of the ninth century (**46**), when structures were taken down and the area eventually covered with domestic refuse. Following this phase of dumping, new buildings were erected throughout the remainder of the ninth century, following the same north-west to south-east alignment as those of earlier periods. A second period of refuse dumping, including great quantities of animal bone, appears to date from the tenth century.

The timber buildings from Flixborough fall within the range that one would expect from a site with seventh- to tenth-century sequences. The protection offered by the midden deposits, however, has led to the preservation of daub fragments, burnt pieces of wood, some prepared, and structural iron fittings as well as a number of unique foundation types. The buildings ranged from 9m x 5.3m in size at the lower end of the scale, up to 19.7m x 6.5m for the largest structure at the site, Building 7. Christopher Loveluck has compared Building 1, with its cobble and sandstone footings, to excavated structures at Middle Anglo-Saxon monasteries, including Hartlepool, Whitby and Whithorn. A small cemetery is associated with the structure, perhaps it is a church or mortuary chapel. The largest structure at the site, Building 7, was also one of the last to be built in the Flixborough sequence. The walls of the building were set into a continuous foundation trench, with timber uprights seated on stone cobble post-settings. The absence of a hearth might suggest an upper storey as proposed for the Long Hall at Cheddar.

The description of the Flixborough site given so far gives little indication of its importance beyond the rare survival of superimposed layers of settlement and occupation debris. The artefacts yielded by the excavations, however, have caused archaeologists to revise completely their criteria for distinguishing between secular and religious settlements of the Middle and Late Anglo-Saxon periods.

Certain of the objects found are of exceptional interest. An inscribed lead plaque listing the names of seven individuals of mixed sex, and a copper-alloy alphabet ring indicate that the residents of the site were at one time or another literate. In addition, a range of silver and copper-alloy *styli* was found (**colour plate 14**), indicating not only the ownership of inscribed artefacts but also the fact that they could have been produced there. A range of industrial activities is attested, including iron- and lead-working. Fine metalworking and, possibly, glass-working are also evidenced. Everyday activities are represented by the splendid hoard of iron tools (**colour plate 15**) found in two lead tanks (**colour plate 16**) and other tools and equipment representing between them the working of wood, leather, textiles and bone. Indeed, the artefactual evidence attests all of the various stages of textile manufacture. Iron spikes represent carding combs, for the preparation of wool or flax, whereas textile manufacture is amply proven by the finding of over 750 loom weights and other equipment including spindle whorls and pin beaters. The carpenters' tools from the hoard are a fine set, with which one could undertake just about every kind of timber work. The hoard itself contained axes, adzes, draw-knives (for taking shavings off) and spoon-bits (for use in a simple drill). Other carpenters tools from the site widen the overall range to include chisels, rasps and wedges.

An examination of the pottery from Flixborough indicates trading links throughout Lincolnshire and into Northamptonshire to the south-west in the eighth and ninth centuries, although regional production could still account for the major variations in the style of domestic pottery at this time. The largest collection of the distinctive Ipswich-Ware pottery to be found north of East Anglia was recovered from the Flixborough

47 *A reconstruction of a thegnly residence with communal hall, ancillary buildings and a bell-tower.* Drawn by Sarah Semple

excavations, which makes an interesting contrast to the relatively small amounts found on certain of the East Anglian sites (see North Elmham below). International contacts are proven by the finding of imported glass vessels, lava querns from the Eiffel region of Germany and a range of ceramics from Belgium and northern France. West Saxon silver pennies of Æthelwulf, Æthelberht and Alfred evidence wider contacts throughout England, although a single penny of Offa represents the only Mercian coin.

Clearly, Flixborough represents a site of intense settlement activity; at points the occupation is of particularly high-status, but at other times the area is used literally as a rubbish dump. If one accepts that such drastic changes can occur within the confines of a settlement, then a change in the character of occupation is also possible. Christopher Loveluck's provisional view is that the site represents a secular estate centre during the earlier and latter stages of its development, but a monastic component to the settlement is possible from the mid-eighth century, when *styli* appear in the archaeological record. It seems that a clear definition between the archaeology of monasteries and secular high-status sites is too blurred to be characterised with any certainty. It should be borne in mind, however, that interpretations based on partially excavated sites are always likely to be rather broad, as archaeologists all too-rarely have the opportunity to select for excavation comparable deposits from different sites. In its broadest context, Flixborough constitutes a 'type site' for an estate centre of the Middle to Late Anglo-Saxon period.

The growth of manorial-type settlements during the tenth and eleventh centuries gave

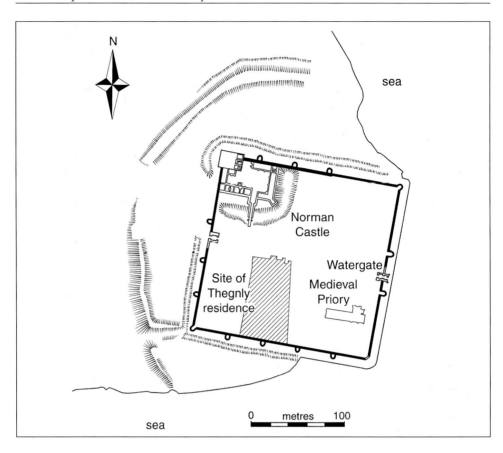

48 *Plan of the Late Roman fort at Portchester Castle, Hampshire showing the location of the Watergate (53), rebuilt in the Late Anglo-Saxon period, and the excavated thegnly residence.* Redrawn from Cunliffe 1976

rise to a new class of settlement, the residences of the *thegnly* classes (**47**). The widespread granting of estates that occurred during this period led to the breaking down of the central importance of former estate centres and to the founding of new ones within each discreet estate. Archaeological excavations have revealed evidence of *thegnly*-type residences from a number of sites and certain of these are explored below. The documentary evidence concerning *thegnly* status and *thegnly* residences has already been presented in Chapters 2 and 3, but the historical evidence agrees well with the range of features and finds from the excavated sites. Two sites in particular, at Portchester Castle in Hampshire and Goltho in Lincolnshire, are considered below in detail. Other sites are known, but an exhaustive review of excavated sites and features is not appropriate here. Reference is made, however, to additional examples and plans of certain of these will suffice.

Barry Cunliffe's excavations at Portchester Castle, Hampshire (**48**) uncovered the core of a *thegnly*-type residence. Portchester Castle itself had seen occupation almost continuously since its construction as a major coastal fortification during the fourth century as one of a chain of eastern seaboard forts known collectively as the forts of the 'Saxon Shore'. In the tenth century the site became an important fort once again, this time as one of the Burghal Hidage defended sites set up by King Alfred and his successors in response to the Viking threat. By the early eleventh century the Manor of Portchester was divided into three separate estates, one of which was presumably centred on the site at Portchester Castle. Coin evidence indicates a relatively wealthy presence at the site during the later ninth century, although by this time structures of eighth-century origin had fallen out of use and the southern part of the excavated site had become a rubbish tip.

The later tenth- and eleventh-century phases present a particularly coherent picture of Anglo-Saxon occupation (**49**). The first period of tenth-century occupation, Phase 5, comprised four buildings, three of which were arranged closely together. The largest Phase 5 building, structure S15, was probably a communal hall. The building measured 12.8m by 9.45m and was furnished with lightly built outer walls and rounded corners with the superstructure supported by three pairs of internal circular posts of between 0.31m and 0.38m in diameter. Each post was set into a square posthole between half and three-quarters of a metre deep. It seems that the principal posts bore the weight of the superstructure, which explains the somewhat light appearance of the outer walls. Quantities of daub suggested to the excavator that there were partitions within the building. Opposing doorways placed midway along the long walls provided entry to the structure. There was no evidence of a hearth, but 27 sherds of pottery were found in backfilled structural features.

To the north of, and in alignment with, what was presumably the main hall lay a post-built structure, S17, measuring 7.9m by 4.9m. The walls had been renewed at least twice after construction, although the floor levels had been lost by erosion and only three sherds of pottery were recovered from two of the postholes. S17 is interpreted as a possible storeroom. To the south-west of the main hall lay building S13, a post in trench construction measuring 12.5m by 6.7m (**50**). This building showed evidence for renewal of the north-west corner. An internal structure, possibly the base for a stepladder, may suggest a building of two storeys; a building with an upper storey is depicted in the Bayeux Tapestry at Bosham, Sussex, where King Harold is shown feasting in a first-floor hall. Furthermore, the *Anglo-Saxon Chronicle* under the year 978 records: 'Here in this year all the foremost councillors of the English race fell down from an upper floor at Calne, but the holy archbishop Dunstan alone was left standing up on a beam; and some were very injured there, and some did not escape it with their life'. Clearly, although the Anglo-Saxons could build two storeys in timber, it was not always done competently! A hearth lay centrally placed toward the west end of Building S13. A small handful of sherds was recovered from its foundation trenches, which also produced quantities of daub.

To the west of this complex lay partially excavated structure S8, a post-built rectangular building, apparently with daub walls to judge by the fragments found nearby. On the north side of S13 an unlined well was dug and further to the north a group of cesspits mark the site of a latrine. A reconstruction of a latrine building from North Elmham, Norfolk gives a good impression of the kind of structure involved (**51**). Rubbish disposal is attested by the finding of pits at the northern and western edges of the site. The above-

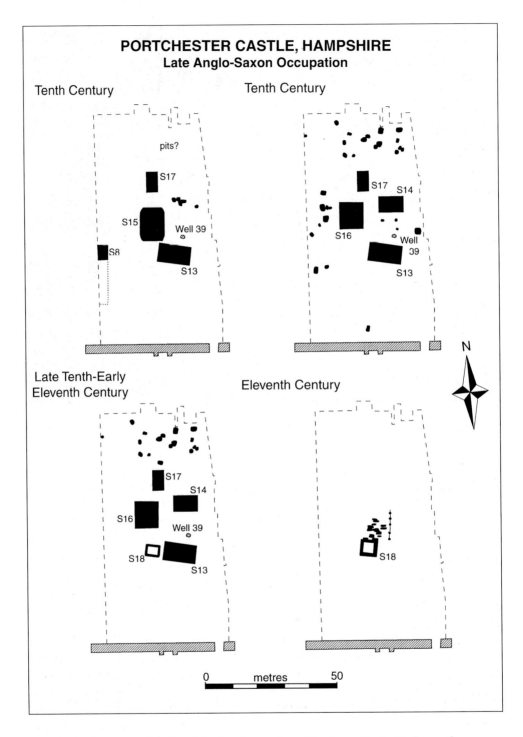

49 *The development and decline of the thegnly complex at Portchester Castle.* Redrawn from Cunliffe 1976

50 *Building S13 at Portchester Castle.* Taken from Cunliffe 1976

mentioned pits were certainly in use during Phase 6 when new structures were erected.

At some point during the tenth century, the earlier hall S15 was replaced with a similar structure S16, the latrines were filled and a timber storehouse, structure S14, erected on the site. Structure S17 was also rebuilt at this time. The well remained in use from the previous phase, whilst rubbish disposal in pits intensified. In general terms the standard of accommodation of the two phases considered above suggests little change in the social and economic position of their occupants.

At the beginning of the eleventh century a lightly built masonry tower (S18), measuring approximately 4m x 5m (**52**), was erected close to the east end of Building S13, otherwise all of the structures from the previous phase remained in use. The tower naturally brings to mind the *thegnly* requirements considered in Chapter 2. There seems no reason to doubt this hypothesis and further evidence for an increase in the status of occupation at the site is indicated by the rebuilding of the Watergate in the pre-existing Roman defensive circuit in stone (**53**). About the middle of the eleventh century the tower S18 was rebuilt on a more substantial scale to about 6m square externally (**52**). The new tower attracted a small cemetery to the north containing some 20 individuals buried without objects of any kind. A post-built boundary on the eastern side of the cemetery suggests that the burial ground was enclosed. By this time the aisled hall (S16) had fallen

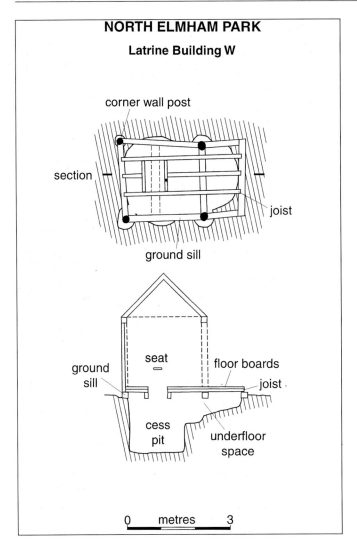

NORTH ELMHAM PARK

Latrine Building W

corner wall post

section

joist

ground sill

seat

ground sill

floor boards

joist

cess pit

underfloor space

0   metres   3

51 *The Late Anglo-Saxon latrine from North Elmham, Norfolk.* Redrawn from Wade-Martins 1980

into disuse, probably with the loss of the other timber buildings of this period. Barry Cunliffe has suggested that the decay of the settlement and the rebuilding and retention of the tower might be related to the building of the Norman Castle in the north-west corner of the Roman fort.

Masonry buildings are rare on domestic sites of the Anglo-Saxon period, but a comparison to the stone structure at Portchester is provided by the results of Brian Davison's excavations at Sulgrave in Northamptonshire. Archaeological excavations at Sulgrave revealed a late tenth- to early eleventh-century residential complex comprising both timber and stone buildings. The west door of the parish church at Sulgrave is triangular headed and probably of Late Anglo-Saxon date. Furthermore, the church is in alignment with the tenth-century hall found at the site and this attribute can be compared to the linear, or axial, planning exhibited particularly strongly at Early and Middle Anglo-Saxon high-status secular sites, but also at Middle and Late Anglo-Saxon ecclesiastical

52 *Building S18 at Portchester Castle, the base of a thegnly tower.* Taken from Cunliffe 1976

centres. The Late Anglo-Saxon '*thegnly* residence' was surrounded with a defensive ditch and can be seen to belong to the same class of '*thegnly* burhs' as Earl's Barton (see Chapter 3, Civil defence) and Goltho, Lincolnshire. Indeed, part of one of Sulgrave's eleventh-century stone buildings may have served as the base for a tower.

Guy Beresford's excavations at Goltho revealed a long sequence of Anglo-Saxon occupation. The earliest occupation comprised a modest farmstead, considered below, but the Late Anglo-Saxon phases represent a further excavated example of a fortified *thegnly* residence (**54**). From about the turn of the ninth and tenth centuries occupation at Goltho took on a rather different appearance. Low status domestic settlement was superseded by the building of a new residential complex comprising successive halls and their attendant buildings arranged around a courtyard area. From at least the tenth century, the main complex of buildings lay within a sub rectangular enclosure, although the parish church lay outside the defensive circuit (**55**). The church of St George at Goltho probably has much earlier origins than the later medieval date suggested by architectural fragments, especially with regard to its proximity and relationship to the *thegnly* complex.

The range of Anglo-Saxon buildings from Goltho compares well with those from Portchester Castle (**56**) among other sites. The ninth- or early tenth-century (Phase 3) hall lay on the south side of the courtyard with kitchen buildings to the east and possible weaving sheds to the north. This basic plan remained during the succeeding Anglo-Saxon Phase 4, although the kitchen ranges were modified and expanded and further rooms were added eastward of a new timber hall.

During Phase 5 at Goltho, the entire complex was surrounded with a substantial sub-circular ditch of defensive proportions, measuring some 110m in length and 100m in

53 *The Watergate at Portchester Castle, perhaps rebuilt during the tenth-century refortification of the site when it was listed in the Burghal Hidage. Note the simple round-headed arch typical of Late Anglo-Saxon masonry architecture.* Taken from Cunliffe 1976

width, which enclosed the area described by the earlier enclosure. Moreover, it is worth noting that the Norman period defences, which lay superimposed upon the Anglo-Saxon manor, occupied a far smaller central area than the Anglo-Saxon residence. The quantity and range of artefacts supports Beresford's contention that the status of the Anglo-Saxon occupation increased with the passage of time. A coin of Cnut found in the kitchen area was associated with large groups of ceramics, with the eleventh-century pottery assemblage exhibiting marked differences with earlier wares. In addition, the range of iron tools compares well with those described in documentary sources as the required 'kit' of an estate centre. Goltho, then, is best seen as site where *thegnly* authority is reflected from the earliest Anglo-Saxon phase, albeit indirectly in the first instance. The later Anglo-Saxon occupation can only represent the accommodation of an individual of *thegnly* status at the heart of an agricultural estate.

By the end of the Anglo-Saxon period the sight of a *thegnly* residence adjacent to a small church with an enclosed cemetery would have been commonplace. The Late Anglo-Saxon masonry church at Alton Barnes, Wiltshire is typical of the kind of small church that would have been found on such estates (**colour plate 18**). Excavations at numerous sites have demonstrated a close physical link between *thegnly* residences and small estate, or proprietary, churches, which later came to serve the parishes we can observe so coherently

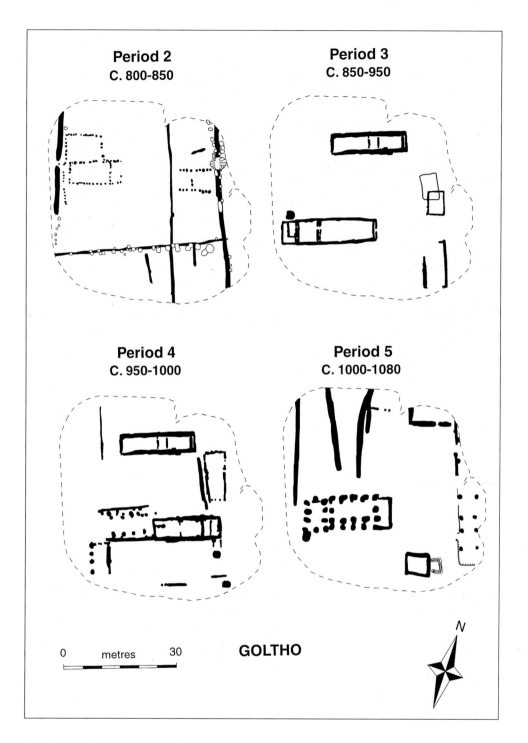

54 *The Middle to Late Anglo-Saxon phases of occupation at Goltho, Lincolnshire.* Redrawn from Beresford 1987

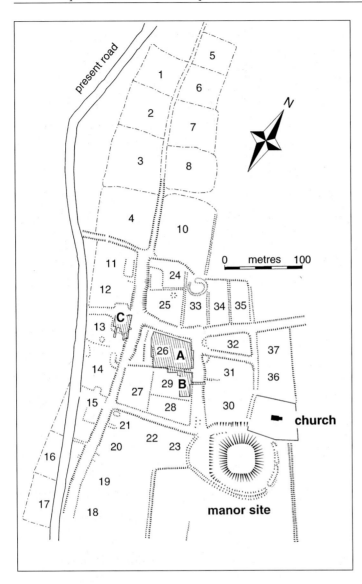

55 *Plan of the deserted village of Goltho showing the relationship of the Anglo-Saxon thegnly residence and the church. Note how the Anglo-Saxon defended enclosure describes a larger area then the Norman castle earthworks that it contained.* Redrawn from Beresford 1987

today. The remarkable excavations at Raunds in Northamptonshire provide a classic, and totally excavated, example of the development of the phenomenon of manor and church (**57**). It is useful here, however, to present the plans of additional contemporary Late Anglo-Saxon sites at Trowbridge, Wiltshire (**58**) and Faccombe Netherton, Hampshire (**59**) for the purposes of comparison. At Raunds, the Saxo-Norman manorial complex was set within a rectilinear enclosure, which was itself the product of continual modification from its establishment in the late seventh century. During the late ninth or early tenth century a small single-celled church was erected outside the east entrance to the manorial enclosure. Until the middle of the tenth century the church lay unenclosed, but the addition of a chancel and the cutting of boundary ditches on the north, east and south sides, coincided with beginning of burial at the site. The redevelopment of the site of the

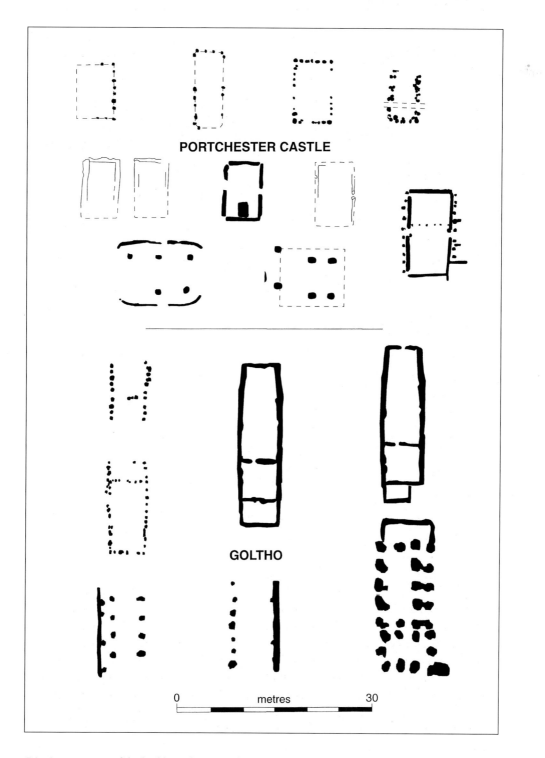

PORTCHESTER CASTLE

GOLTHO

0   metres   30

56 *A comparison of the buildings from Portchester Castle and Goltho.* Redrawn from Cunliffe 1976 and Beresford 1987

RAUNDS FURNELLS, NORTHAMPTONSHIRE

Saxo-Norman Manorial Complex

cornbrash quarries

quarry pits

aisled hall

0 metres 30

57 *The Saxo-Norman manorial complex at Raunds, Northamptonshire. Note the relationship between the thegnly residence and the church.* Redrawn from Boddington 1996

church and churchyard to secular use in the late twelfth or early thirteenth century serves to indicate that manor/church arrangements were not necessarily permanent. Other short-lived churches are known, for example that at Potterne in Wiltshire, and some element of continual settlement mobility should be allowed for. Indeed, the deserted villages of the later medieval period are a testimony to the ongoing process of settlement and landscape development, and deserted sites need not necessarily be viewed in the light of catastrophic social and economic change.

The dwellings of farm workers could also be found close by the *thegnly* complex with peasant houses located within plots of land set out under lordly authority. With variations, this form of settlement existed in many regions of England and the following section explores the archaeology of rural life.

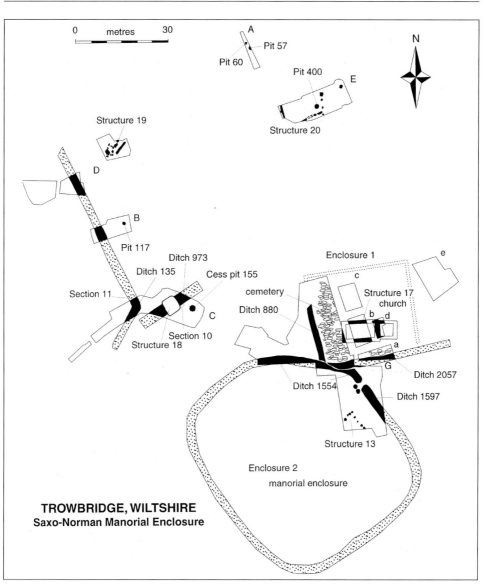

58 *The Saxo-Norman manorial complex at Trowbridge, Wiltshire.* Redrawn from Graham and Davies 1993

Villages and farmsteads

Excavated settlements of the Middle and Late Anglo-Saxon periods are still relatively few. Besides the high-status sites considered above, there are a small number of lower status settlements that have been archaeologically investigated. The importance of these sites is principally that they represent the origins of village communities in England. The increasingly formalised plan forms of excavated settlements along with a consideration of the artefactual materials allows a picture to be formed of the effects of wider social

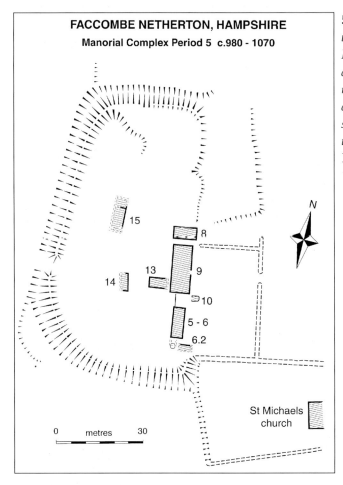

FACCOMBE NETHERTON, HAMPSHIRE

Manorial Complex Period 5 c.980 - 1070

15

8

13

14   9

10

5 - 6

6.2

N

St Michaels
church

0   metres   30

59 *The Late Anglo-Saxon thegnly residence at Faccombe Netherton, Hampshire. In common with other enclosed manorial complexes, the church and churchyard are seemingly an afterthought to the residential buildngs.* Redrawn from Fairbrother 1990

developments such as the evolution of the English kingdoms on the countryside. The loose groupings of farmsteads, with little evidence for hierarchy, which existed from the fifth century in most regions, emerged from the seventh century political melting pot as largely tied communities. Middle and Late Anglo-Saxon rural settlements, excluding upland sites, were frequently characterised by planned layouts, including boundary ditches around individual properties and in some cases around the settlement itself as at Avebury in Wiltshire (**60**).

The earliest Anglo-Saxon occupation discovered during Guy Beresford's excavations at Goltho is represented by a modest farmstead with two broadly contemporary timber buildings set within a rectilinear arrangement of boundary features (**54**). The buildings are of simple post-built type and compare well with buildings from earlier Anglo-Saxon settlements such as Mucking in Essex and Chalton in Hampshire as well as with those from contemporary Middle and Late Anglo-Saxon sites. Both structures were formed of upright posts set in individual postholes between 0.6m and 0.9m apart, with internal divisions within the buildings.

Building 1 was the earlier of the two structures and measured 10.8m long, 5.4m wide

60 *A reconstruction of Late Anglo-Saxon Avebury.* Drawn by Sarah Semple

at the east end and 4.8m wide at the west. Opposed doorways lay to the east of the partition. Building 2 was 13.2m in length and bow-sided in plan, being 5.8m wide in the middle, but only 5.1m at either end. The partitioned area lay at the east end of the building and defined a narrow space some 2.5m in width. Entry to the building was achieved via opposing doorways toward the west end. A fenced yard to the north of Building 2 contained two rectangular stone hearths associated with a layer of slag suggesting smithing activity. Beresford has proposed that a covering of timber-laced clay would have concealed the wall timbers of both buildings. The lack of evidence for timber uprights at either end of Building 1 is not an uncommon feature during the Middle and Late Anglo-Saxon periods. A comparable example of such a building can be found at the royal palace of Cheddar where Building Z lacked evidence for its east wall. No evidence for hearths was found inside either of the Goltho buildings, as the floors had been erased by later activity on the site. Occupation deposits associated with Building 2 in particular, however, attest to domestic occupation.

The pattern of rectilinear ditched enclosures, within which the buildings were set, gives an impression of authoritative planning and of the development of concepts of property associated with production and taxation, these aspects are considered later. The physical pattern of the property divisions suggests that the rectangular plots were laid out in respect to an existing trackway at the east of the site. The major east-west boundary within the excavated area is seen as a division between two farmsteads, with the majority of the settlement archaeology related to the northernmost farmstead. The first phase of this boundary feature took the form of a ditch and was contemporary with the occupation of Building 1. The boundary was subsequently replaced on the same line with timber posts at about the same time that Building 2 was erected.

Deposits of Middle Anglo-Saxon pottery included so-called Torksey and Maxey-type wares, although the majority of the products were probably produced in Lincoln. The range of pottery associated with the Goltho farmstead comprised 65% cooking pots and 25% bowls. Other vessels including a Torksey Ware bowl and two Stamford Ware pitchers represented the finer pots in use. Beresford has suggested a date range of *c*.800–*c*.850 for the Middle Saxon occupation at Goltho, although there are some grounds for a slightly later dating of the farmstead, perhaps toward the end of the ninth century or even later. Apart from the remains of oxen, pigs and sheep, there was no evidence to indicate whether the inhabitants of the site were involved predominantly in either pastoral or arable farming, although a mixture is likely.

The change of use of the site during the later ninth century to a high-status fortified residence brings a rather sharper focus to the lifestyle, responsibilities and authority of the *thegnly* classes who had probably determined the property divisions between the farmsteads of the earlier phase.

At North Elmham in Norfolk, Peter Wade-Martins has excavated a settlement associated with the important ecclesiastical centre there, probably the Anglo-Saxon episcopal centre of the diocese of Elmham. There is evidence for both Middle and Late Anglo-Saxon activity in the form of properties and houses and other features such as wells. The earliest phase of Anglo-Saxon occupation dates to the eighth century as indicated by the presence in residual contexts of two eighth-century coins, or *sceattas*, and by a series of radiocarbon dates from animal remains found in the major boundary ditches that determined the layout of the settlement until the late ninth century. It is possible that a few buildings existed prior to the establishment of the planned settlement, but it is the three parallel ditches which stand out as primary features in the Middle Anglo-Saxon period (**61**). Buildings associated with the earliest planned phase were of timber, as at Goltho, but the North Elmham structures used a different construction technique; the placing of timber uprights in foundation trenches as opposed to individual postholes. In some cases, the impressions left by squared posts were recorded. A further point of comparison with the Goltho farmsteads lies in the juxtaposition between houses and properties and a thoroughfare or street. At North Elmham, the two easternmost north-south ditches appear to define a route-way against which properties were laid out, with individual structures at both sites placed end on to the street. The first phase at Elmham also seems to represent fragments of at least two separate properties. Northern and southern properties appear to have been separated by a boundary ditch, with a substantial house measuring 13m by 6.2m occupying the northern plot.

A greater area of the southern plot was explored, which provided evidence for production in the form of a bakehouse situated to the south of a house that had been rebuilt once and then modified. The bakehouse itself measured 5.4m by 6m internally with an oven in the centre of the room. The oven had been rebuilt a least three times and

61 *The Middle Anglo-Saxon settlement (Period 1) at North Elmham, Norfolk. Note the substantial boundary features.* Redrawn from Wade-Martins 1980

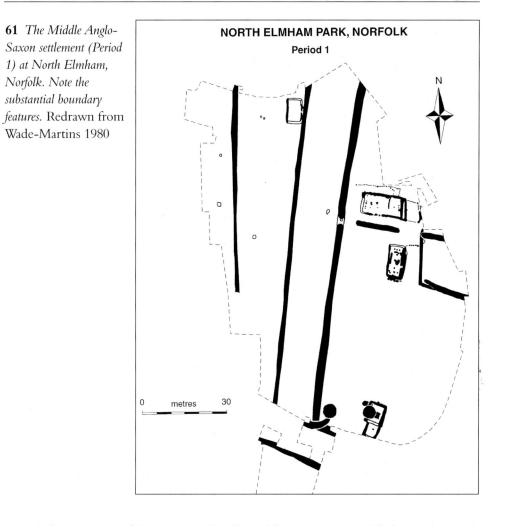

extended occupation of the structure is indicated by an extension added onto the south side of the bakehouse after its initial construction. To the west of the bakehouse lay a substantial well formed of two circular, straight-sided wooden cylinders surmounted by a square shaft which rose up to at least ground level. The bakehouse was eventually abandoned and a further timber-lined well was dug in its place in about 830 according to dendrochronological and radiocarbon dating. At about this time, the house in the northern property was extended to the east, the house in the southern property was rebuilt and boundaries were modified at the eastern edge of the site. Further evidence for economic activity was revealed in the form of animal remains, which indicated a predominance of sheep over cattle.

The presence of the prolific Ipswich Ware pottery industry in East Anglia from the later seventh century led to widespread consumption of its products in both the eastern counties and beyond. The quantity of Ipswich-type ceramics from all the Middle Anglo-Saxon features at North Elmham is surprisingly low at 114 sherds. The relative scarcity in the earliest phases, however, can now be seen to support a later date for the origins of its production rather than an unusual aspect of ceramic use at the site. A single sherd of so-called Tating Ware, probably manufactured in the Rhineland or Northern France during the late eighth to early ninth century, may well reflect the ecclesiastical associations of the North Elmham settlement.

A further excavated Middle Anglo-Saxon settlement worthy of attention is that at Wicken Bonhunt in Essex excavated by Keith Wade and Andrew Rogerson. The site faces southward down a gentle slope toward a river and the locale has seen intermittent human occupation since the Mesolithic period (the Middle Stone Age). During the late sixth or early seventh century an Anglo-Saxon phase of occupation began which was to last until the time of the Norman Conquest, with settlement continuing on into the medieval period. The earliest Anglo-Saxon activity was represented by a series of pits and ditches, but no structures were found. Ceramics associated with this early phase were handmade and sand-tempered, very much in the tradition of local Early Anglo-Saxon wares.

About 700 major re-planning took place when a substantial boundary ditch was dug running north to south across the site. A further boundary was dug to the west of the early ditch and parallel with it and probably represents a phase of settlement expansion. Both ditches contained quantities of Ipswich Ware in their filling, which provides a broad date for the beginning of this phase. The excavated area contained at least 28 structures of several distinct periods arranged either at right angles to, or parallel with, the north-south boundary ditches (**62**). The usual range of construction techniques were present, including individual posts set into the ground, short foundation trenches with settings of individual posts and continuous foundation trenches. The buildings themselves ranged widely in terms of floor area from 36m sq. to 130m sq. Only the largest excavated structure (Building V) was found to have had a hearth, although plough damage almost certainly accounts for the loss of floors, hearths and other features from individual buildings.

While evidence for the function of buildings is largely lost, the range of artefacts and ecofacts recovered from the principal boundary ditches revealed much about the economic and social patterns of the site's inhabitants. Some 70% of the pottery assemblage is formed of Ipswich Ware, whilst 20% per cent comprises local handmade pottery. Of the greatest significance, however, is the remaining 10%, which constitutes continental imports. Imported wares appear largely French in origin, with Carolingian burnished grey and black ware pitchers forming the larger part, but a rare find included a three-handled, red-painted pitcher in Beauvais Ware.

Two wells were found belonging to the Middle Anglo-Saxon phase. Well 1 was lined with wicker held in place by four corner posts, whereas Well 2 was built first with oak planks set behind corner posts, but subsequently with the planks mortised into posts at the corners. A radiocarbon determination from Well 2 provided a date of 830, give or take 50 years.

An insight into the economic background of the settlement is suggested by both structural and artefactual evidence. The large post-built structure N, situated in the north eastern part of the site is interpreted as a granary, whilst the sorting of soil samples from deposits of Middle and Late Anglo-Saxon date suggested an economy based on wheat, oats, barley, peas and beans. A large quantity of bird bones recovered from the earliest north-south ditch was found to comprise a great number of individuals including 295 fowl, 228 geese, 35 ducks, 10 doves and one peacock. Keith Wade has suggested that the large proportion of adult fowl is indicative of egg production, whereas the wild birds reveal varied surroundings including marshland, woodland and farmland. The early boundary ditch also contained a rather strange but significant deposit of the bones of larger animals. The assemblage represented the normal variety of species but in a very selective manner. Six hundred pigs were identified, but mostly the finds were of heads, in addition to 200 cattle and 100 sheep.

The range of equipment necessary for textile production, including an iron linen heckle, bone thread-pickers, spindle whorls and loom weights was found at Wicken, which ultimately limits the activities represented by the archaeological evidence to the everyday. The presence of imported ceramics is of interest given that imported finds probably entered the country via one of the newly emerging international trading centres, or *wics* discussed in Chapter 5. In the case of Wicken Bonhunt, Ipswich seems a likely port of entry if the large quantities of Ipswich Ware recovered from the excavations are anything to go by. London and Hamwic, however, dealt more with French products, which might imply links between Wicken and either of these two *wic* sites.

After a break in occupation, settlement at Wicken was revived in the eleventh century by the setting out of four adjacent plots of land delimited by north-south ditches (**63**). One of the plots contained a structure at its southern end and the entire plan is reminiscent of the regular plans of many later medieval villages. The southern limit of the new plots was defined by the northern limit of a rectangular enclosure. To the east the small, probably proprietary, church of St Helen may have come into existence during this phase when, as at Raunds, boundaries became more extensive with the addition of a church and cemetery to a *thegnly* residence.

A fitting contrast to the sites laid out in an open fashion is the recently excavated, but not yet fully published, Middle to Late Anglo-Saxon site from Bramford parish on the outskirts of modern Ipswich (**64**). The importance of Ipswich during this period is not in doubt and is covered in Chapter 5, but the Bramford site surely fell within its hinterland. The first point of departure from the sites so far considered is the existence of an enclosure ditch around the settlement. The ditch was broad, up to 2.8m, and, in places, up to 1.4m deep. The area described by this enclosure was 'D'-shaped and measured approximately 100m by 80m. Within the perimeter, the internal area was divided into three plots defined by shallow ditches, but which probably held fences or hedges. The northern plot was occupied by Building 1, which measured 11.5m by 7m and was built using a combination of individual postholes and foundation trenches. There were opposing doorways midway along the long walls but, typically, all traces of former floors or hearths had been erased from the site by later events. Two silver *sceattas* from a large rubbish pit provide dating evidence for Middle Anglo-Saxon domestic occupation. Of particular importance with regard to the northern plot is the finding of a small cemetery containing 16 bodies as this indicates that inhuming the dead in private graveyards was still possible well into the Christian period. Very little of the western plot survived, but the southern area was found to contain Building 2, a predominantly post-built structure

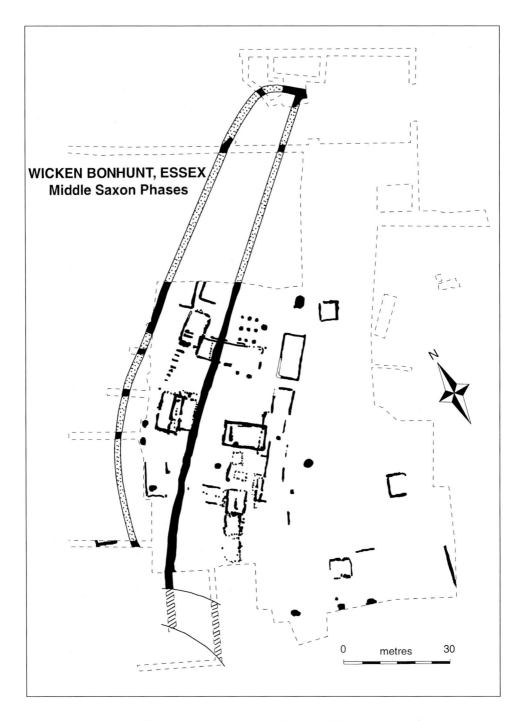

WICKEN BONHUNT, ESSEX
Middle Saxon Phases

0   metres   30

62 *The Middle Anglo-Saxon settlements at Wicken Bonhunt, Essex. Note the similarity with North Elmham.* Redrawn from Wade 1980

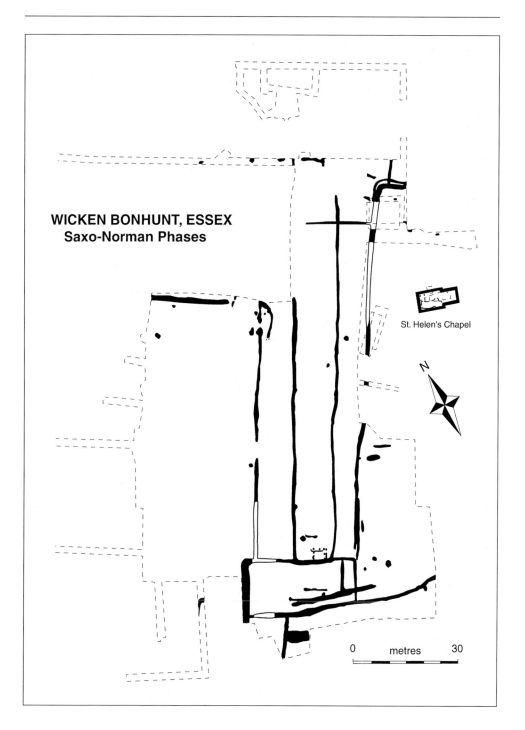

WICKEN BONHUNT, ESSEX
Saxo-Norman Phases

St. Helen's Chapel

0   metres   30

63 *The Saxo-Norman settlement at Wicken Bonhunt, Essex showing major property boundaries.*
Redrawn from Wade 1980

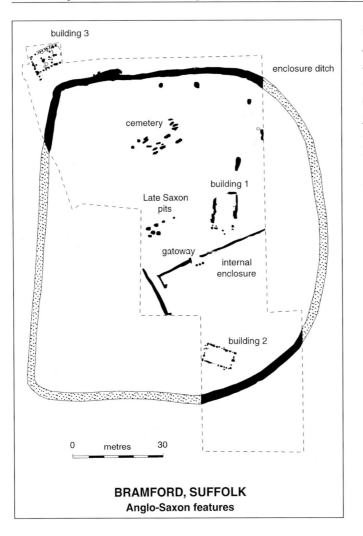

building 3

enclosure ditch

cemetery

building 1

Late Saxon pits

gateway

internal enclosure

building 2

0   metres   30

BRAMFORD, SUFFOLK
Anglo-Saxon features

64 *The Middle to Late Anglo-Saxon enclosed settlement at Bramford, Suffolk. Note the cemetery in the northern plot.* Redrawn from Nenk, Margeson and Hurley 1996 after Suffolk County Council

measuring 9.3m by 5.5m. There were two gateways between the northern and southern properties, including one of a three-post type commonly found on Late Anglo-Saxon settlement sites including Cheddar (see below).

Bramford demonstrates the existence of enclosed settlements at this period but there are indications of others at sites such as Higham Ferrers in Northamptonshire. Fieldwalking, excavation and geophysical survey at the latter site revealed a substantial quantity of ceramics of Early, Middle and Late Anglo-Saxon date, which corresponded broadly with an area described by an oval ditched enclosure (**65**). Distributions of finds suggest that during the Early to Middle Anglo-Saxon periods, settlement was located to the west of the enclosure but that by the Late Anglo-Saxon period occupation had spread over much of the interior. The full details are not yet available but the evidence is sufficient to indicate a greater consideration for the division of landscape.

An enclosed settlement with a somewhat different morphology is the seventh- to ninth-century site at Riby Cross Roads, Lincolnshire. Here, an agglomeration of enclosed

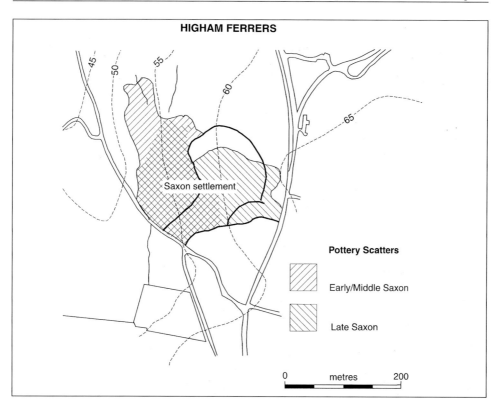

65 *The Anglo-Saxon enclosed settlement at Higham Ferrers, Northamptonshire.* Redrawn from Shaw 1991

plots of land forms what can only be described as a village-type plan-form (**66**). A recent review by Stuart Wrathmell has shown that later medieval villages might be formed just as easily by the development of routeways between separate plots as by the setting out of properties along an existing route. The Riby settlement provides an early example of this process, arrested at a stage rarely visualised by archaeologists.

There is a good historical context for the appearance of boundary features during the seventh century. Ine's laws contain a series of clauses concerned with the responsibilities of farmers with regard to maintaining fences and enclosures. Although the code relates to the West Saxon kingdom, the archaeological evidence indicates geographically broad concerns amongst agricultural communities for the necessity of property division. Ine's laws state that: 'A ceorl's homestead must be fenced winter and summer' and that, 'if ceorls have a common meadow or other land divided in shares to fence, and some have fenced their portion and some have not, and [if cattle] eat up their common crops or grass, those who are responsible for the gap are to go and pay to the others, who have fenced their part, compensation for the damage that has been done there'.

The Kentish laws of King Wihtred are contemporary with those of Ine and, although there are close similarities in certain matters, there is no mention of the need to introduce

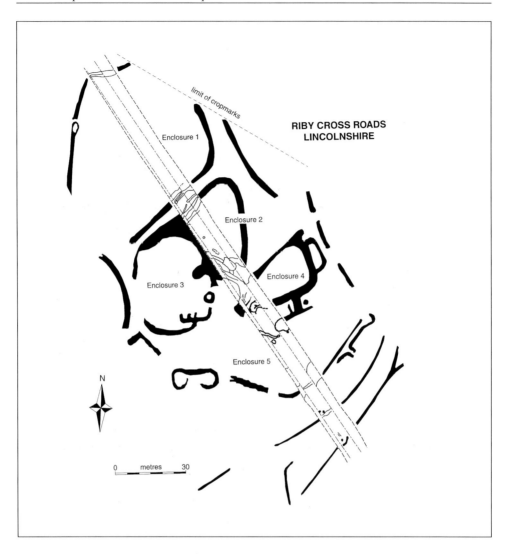

66 *Plan of part of the Middle Anglo-Saxon settlement at Riby Crossroads, Lincolnshire. Note how enclosures define pathways in contrast to sites such as North Elmham (**61**) and Wicken Bonhunt (**62**) where linear boundaries appear to have determined the settlement form.* Redrawn from Steedman 1994

boundaries into the landscape. Perhaps this due to the continued existence of small hedged fields laid out at an earlier period in contrast to much of the Wessex landscape whose boundaries were less well-defined and in many cases much more ancient.

The settlements described above were largely chosen because they represent large-scale excavations that have revealed entire properties, or at least substantial fragments of these. At other sites where Middle Anglo-Saxon settlement remains have been found, limited or dispersed excavation areas often intensify the problems of interpretation. A prime example

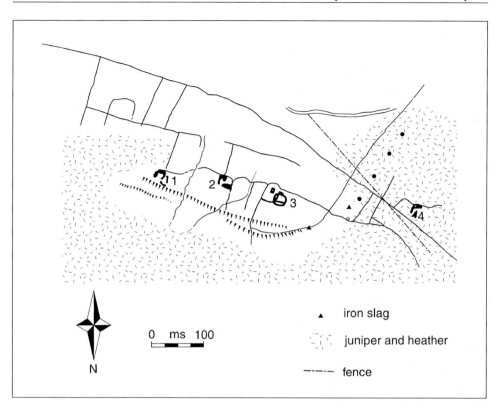

67 *Plan of the Middle Anglo-Saxon upland settlement at Simy Folds, Upper Teesdale, Co. Durham. The rectilinear field system surrounding the settlement foci (Sites 1-4) is of probable prehistoric origin.* Redrawn from Coggins, Fairless and Batey 1983

of such a scenario can be found at Wharram Percy in North Yorkshire.

The Wharram project is principally known for its concern with the development of the later medieval village in England, but over 40 years excavations at the site have led to the discovery of both Middle and Late Anglo-Saxon settlement remains over a wide area. Beyond the fact that occupation is attested, it is not possible to examine aspects of settlement development to the same extent as it is at Goltho or North Elmham. Julian Richards has recently reviewed the evidence for Middle Anglo-Saxon Wharram. The evidence of eighth-century carved stonework, in combination with finds of *sceatta* coins, evidence for smithing and Tating-Type Ware, has led Richards to suggest the existence of an early ecclesiastical complex. Given the difficulties of separating secular and ecclesiastical settlements on archaeological grounds, along with the piecemeal picture of Middle Anglo-Saxon settlement remains presented by the excavations, it is difficult to make further progress towards an understanding of Wharram's early development. Ultimately, it is only by large-scale open area excavation that we can hope to understand settlements of our period.

An example of the use of pre-existing field patterns is provided by the upland settlement

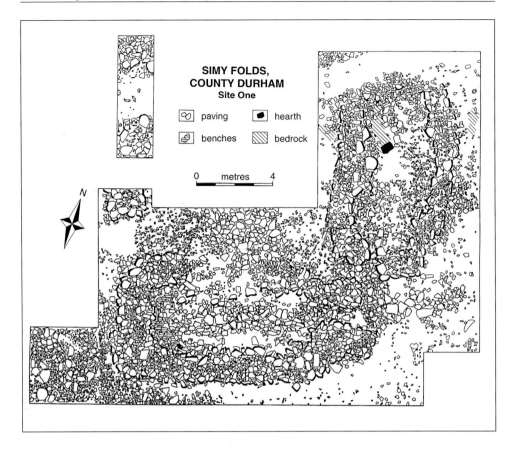

68 *Simy Folds Site 1. Drystone-walled structures arranged around a courtyard. Compare to similar houses in upland areas at Gauber High Pasture (70) and Mawgan Porth (71).* Redrawn from Coggins, Fairless and Batey 1983

of Simy Folds in County Durham. Here, a series of dry-stone buildings were set within a prehistoric pattern of small fields defined by dry-stone walls (**67**). Although no datable artefacts were found during excavations between 1976 and 1981, radiocarbon determinations taken from hearth deposits suggest occupation during the mid- to late eighth century. The buildings themselves were basic in terms of layout and architecture. Excavations were made in four areas strung east to west in a line along the bench of limestone upon which the settlement lies. Site 1 revealed two stone buildings set at right angles to each other (**68**). Building 1 lay to the south and west of Building 2. Internally the structure measured 9m by 4m and it was entered via a doorway at the east end where an area of paving also served the entrance to Building 2. Building 2 was 1m shorter than Building 1, although both structures were provided with hearths and stone benches indicating domestic settlement. Buildings at Sites 2 and 3 were divided into two rooms, in similar proportions to contemporary timber buildings. Building 3 from Site 2 was furnished with a hearth on a raised platform to the south of a masonry wall separating the two rooms (**69**). Smithing activity in the form of slag and other metalworking residues was recovered from all of the excavated sites with a particular concentration found at Site 1. Such domestic smithing is comparable with the evidence for metalworking from Goltho. A sample of charcoal from a cutting through a slag heap at Site 2 produced a radiocarbon date centring on 820.

Although a balanced agricultural regime is arguable on the basis of the evidence from Simy Folds, it seems more likely that such an upland settlement would have been far better suited to a predominantly pastoral economy. This does not exclude the possibility that the community there could have grown all of their cereal requirements. Analysis of ancient pollen preserved in peat deposits to the north of the excavated site allowed cereal pollen to be identified in a context of open grassland with relatively low levels of tree pollen. Because cereal pollen tends to be deposited within a few hundred metres from its source, it seems that the Middle Anglo-Saxon occupation at Simy Folds was responsible for its production. A comparable site to Simy Folds is that at Gauber High Pasture, Ribblehead in North Yorkshire. Here the excavations revealed three rectangular buildings arranged around a yard (**70**) with activity by at least the later ninth century attested by the finding of a coin.

Upland settlements of the type described above constitute specialised farming communities. It is easy to imagine that such settlements acted in response to their frequently harsh environments, but the evidence for cereal cultivation from Simy Folds suggests a high degree of economic self-sufficiency, although the principal role of these sites is likely to have been pastoral.

Overall, there can be little doubt that the increasingly complex society revealed by the documentary record is readily paralleled by the settlement archaeology of the period. During the Late Anglo-Saxon period, rural settlements very much follow the lead set during the preceding centuries, although the nature of sites is more diverse with regard to plan form.

From the late ninth and tenth centuries *thegnly* estate centres with proprietary, or parish churches, developed alongside ecclesiastical estate centres. Scholars are in general agreement that there is likely to be little if any difference between the daily circumstances of those who worked on such estates and this is borne out by the archaeological evidence.

At sites such as North Elmham the character of the settlement archaeology changes during the late ninth and tenth centuries. The formally laid out Middle-Saxon settlement at North Elmham was replaced by what was to become by the tenth century, a *thegnly*-type residence. This sequence bears obvious comparisons with Goltho.

Mawgan Porth in Cornwall provides a rare example of the nature of settlement on the fringes of the Late Anglo-Saxon world. The nature of occupation is somewhat different from that found in the rest of England at this time, but the site does serve as an important reminder of issues of regional variation and identity in relation to archaeological remains. The settlement lies on a slope overlooking the sea on the north coast of Cornwall. Besides the settlement remains at Mawgan Porth, a small cemetery was excavated, which is apparently not associated with a church of any kind. Further to the east, in Wessex, churches were being established in increasing numbers on rural estates, although a growing number of small 'field cemeteries' of the Middle and Late

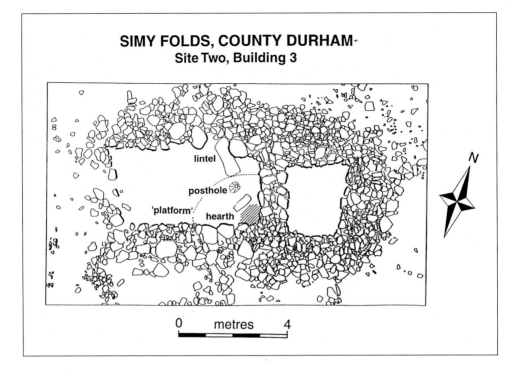

69 *Simy Folds Site 2, Building 3, showing a two-roomed drystone building with a hearth.*
Redrawn from Coggins, Fairless and Batey 1983

Anglo-Saxon period are now being recognised. It now seems that the Middle Anglo-Saxons continued to bury in small rural cemeteries without churches, merely ceasing to inhume their dead with objects during the course of the seventh century. The minster cemeteries, so it seems, did not have a total monopoly on burial; a situation borne out by the Bramford site discussed above.

The structural evidence from Mawgan Porth is of particular interest as the buildings belong to the so-called 'long-house' tradition more familiar to students of twelfth century and later rural settlements. The long house is defined as a structure where humans and animals share the same accommodation with a cross-passage separating the two. The three excavated dwellings at Mawgan Porth comprised a number of separate structures arranged around courtyards. A description of one of these, Courtyard House 1 will serve as an example (**71**). The main house, Room 1, was built with dry-stone-faced walls, with a core of slate rubble and earth, probably originally to full height. The roof was most likely covered with turf, which was probably the case with the other buildings at the site. The structure measured 10.1m in length and 4.3m in width and contained a wide range of structural features including opposed doorways midway along the north and south walls and an entrance at the east end opening onto the courtyard area; the north door provided entry into Room 2. The western part of the room was partitioned from the rest. The presence of a posthole in the central part of this space and

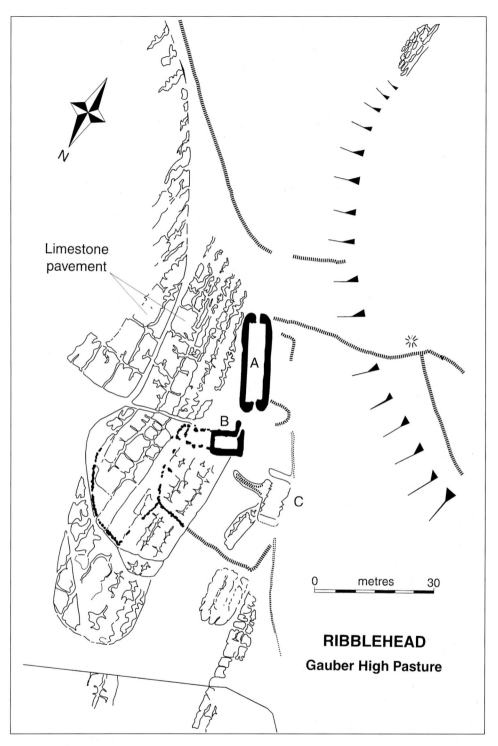

70 *Plan of the ninth-century settlement at Gauber High Pasture, Ribblehead, North Yorkshire.*
Redrawn from King 1978

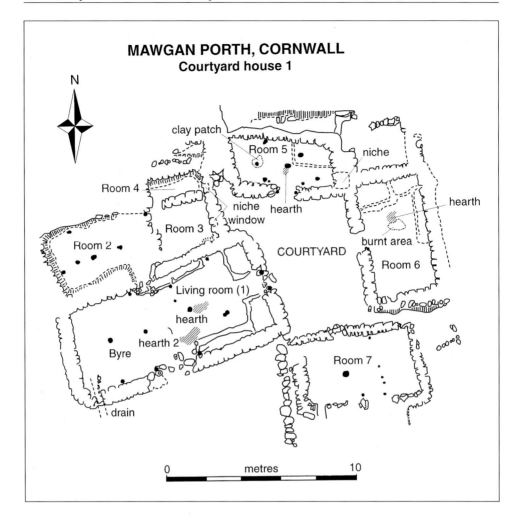

71 *Courtyard House 1 from the Late Anglo-Saxon settlement at Mawgan Porth, Cornwall.* Redrawn from Bruce-Mitford 1997

of a drain in the south-west corner of the room all suggest that Room 1 served as both an animal byre and as a residence. The eastern part of the room possessed a central hearth and another adjacent to the south door. A number of slab-lined slot-like features cut into the natural bedrock up against the inside walls of the room further indicate a domestic function. A further six rooms were found to the north and east of Room 1. Two of these buildings, Rooms 5 and 6, contained hearths, but little indication of the presence of animals. It seems that each of the three Courtyard Houses at Mawgan Porth functioned as individual farmsteads probably housing extended families, although such a multiplicity of hearths might suggest some degree of independence within the context of the settlement unit.

The dating of occupation at Mawgan Porth is reliant on ceramics for its early development. A comparison of the ceramics from Courtyard House 3 with other sites in the region suggests a ninth century origin for the settlement, although a coin of Æthelred the Unready, dated to between 990 and 995, was recovered in one of the latest occupation contexts at the site.

A large quantity of stone implements including hammers, smoothers, sharpening stones and spindle whorls illustrate how the inhabitants of the settlement drew largely on local resources for their tools and equipment. Indeed, the economy of the site has been described as one of 'stone and bone'. Metal objects were rare, with a total absence of dress-fittings, although ceramics were consumed in notable quantities with some 2000 sherds having been found. Cooking pots of so-called 'bar-lip' or 'bar-lug' type formed the majority of the assemblage. Animal remains from the site comprised a variety of species with a predominance of Celtic ox and sheep or goat. Dogs and cats were present along with horses, with the remains of a probable fighting cock providing information about recreational behaviour.

The heartlands of Late Anglo-Saxon Wessex, including Berkshire, Wiltshire and Hampshire, were characterised by a landscape of largely nucleated villages, such as Raunds, operating as estate centres for the multiplicity of small agricultural estates born out of the fragmentation of large Middle Anglo-Saxon estates during the tenth century. Michael Costen, however, has studied tenth century charter boundaries relating to Wiltshire, Dorset and Somerset which clearly demonstrate that the settlement geography of these regions was far more diverse, with a multiplicity of isolated homesteads lying on or near the boundaries of estates. The charters use a range of terms to describe dwelling places. Examples from the bounds include the *olde wested* 'the old west steading' at Sturminster and the *hus* 'house' at Compton Abbas, both in Dorset, and *Æthelferthes setle* 'Aethelferth's dwelling place' at East Overton in Wiltshire.

The archaeology of such sites is little known, although excavations on chalk downland at Easton Lane to the north-east of Winchester in the early 1980s revealed evidence of such a site on the parish boundary between Easton and Winnall. Machine stripping revealed a large rectangular enclosure measuring 40m in length and 16.5m in width, located on a north facing slope (**72**). A shallow but well-defined ditch described the enclosure with a narrow entrance at its eastern end. The ditch was observed to have cut through an earlier, but probably Late Anglo-Saxon, pit. During the life of the settlement, the enclosure passed out of use and this is demonstrated by the cutting of a later pit through the infilled enclosure ditch.

On the basis of size, the excavators wisely dismissed the possibility that the structure was roofed and it is perhaps best seen as a storage place for stock or produce. Indications that the enclosure was attended, perhaps with a resident farm worker, are provided by domestic finds from the filling of the enclosure ditch and from a series of Late Anglo-Saxon pits; one found within the west end of the enclosure and the remainder to the north-west. Overall the quantity of ceramics was small at 216 sherds, but sufficient to support the notion of settlement activity at the site. The contents of the enclosure ditch included three fragments of Mayen Lava (a common import from North Germany used to manufacture domestic querns stones) and a possible loom weight fragment. The majority of the diagnostic pottery finds were derived from the ditch and included a rim

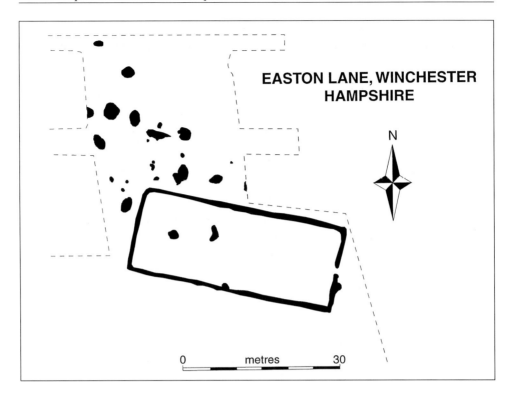

72 *The Late Anglo-Saxon enclosure, probably a sheep pen, and associated pits at Easton Lane, Winchester, Hampshire.* Redrawn from Fasham, Farwell and Whinney 1989

decorated with characteristic Late Anglo-Saxon 'pie-crust' decoration. The contents of the pits was largely limited to animal bones, but included the base of a vessel. Of particular significance is the composition of the animal bone assemblage, which comprised largely of sheep. Mark Maltby, who analysed the animal remains, has suggested a population composed predominantly of breeding ewes and that the presence of at least four foetal or new-born lambs amongst the flock indicates occupation during winter or early spring. It might be suggested that occupation at the Easton Lane site was seasonal in nature, perhaps connected with grazing patterns of the Late Anglo-Saxon Easton estate's flocks.

Production and economy

The practical considerations and material requirements of the Later Anglo-Saxon estate are described in certain Old English texts, sometimes in remarkable detail. We have already noted the tenth century promotion law, *Geþyncðo*, which gives a broad outline of certain of the principal requirements of the estate owner or *thegn*, but other texts, known as estate memoranda give much more detail with regard to seasonal and even daily considerations. One tenth- or eleventh-century estate memorandum provides an extensive list of the events of the farming year and of the tools and equipment required on a busy farm. The following excerpts will suffice.

> In May and June and July in summer one may: harrow, carry out manure, procure sheep-hurdles, shear sheep, build, repair, construct in timber, cut wood, weed, make folds, construct a fish-weir and mill; at harvest time reap, in August and September and October: mow, cut wood, gather in many crops, thatch, cover over and clean out folds, make ready cow-sheds and also pig-sties before too severe a winter come to the manor...

Amongst the bewildering array of equipment described by the memorandum are:

> ...axe, adze, bill, awl, plane, saw, spoke-shave, tie-hook, auger, mattock, crow-bar, share, coulter; and also goad-iron, scythe, sickle, hoe, spade, shovel, woad-trowel, barrow, broom, mallet, rake, fork, ladder, curry-comb and shears, fire tongs, steelyard; and many cloth-working tools: flax-lines, spindle, reel, yarn-winder, stoddle, beams, press, comb, card, weft, woof, wool-comb, roller, slay, crank, shuttle, seam-pegs, shears, needle, beater.

> And if he has skilled workmen he must assist them with tools: miller, shoe-maker, lead-founder, and other workers — each occupation will itself show what pertains to it; there is no man that can enumerate all the tools which one must have.

Much of the equipment of the rural estate described here is made of organic materials and is therefore poorly represented in the archaeological record, although an early-medieval wooden spade has been found in Durham. Hoards of iron tools, such as that from Flixborough, reflect the day-to-day maintenance required on a large estate, building and mending all manner of things. A significant number of the sites considered in this chapter has revealed evidence for metalworking, although this ranges from domestic ironworking to specialised industry.

There is a tendency for industrial production to be linked to high-status sites, particularly the secular centres as at Tamworth, capital of the Mercians, where a remarkable water mill of horizontal-wheeled type, dated to the ninth century, was excavated in the 1970s. At Ramsbury in Wiltshire, industrial iron-furnaces dated to the late eighth and early ninth centuries have been excavated, which most likely operated within the sphere of royal influence. The evidence for iron-working from Cheddar, for example, conforms to this pattern.

Prior to the tenth century it seems that Anglo-Saxon field systems were adaptations of pre-existing field patterns, or either they were very similar to them. Certainly, there is no clear evidence for a characteristic 'Anglo-Saxon' field until the advent of open field systems probably from the tenth century. Open field agriculture relies on the co-operation of a community in order to maximise yields and profit margins. The move toward nucleation is still imperfectly understood, but the archaeological evidence that is available suggests that ridge and furrow was in existence as a field type at least by the late eleventh century, owing to its discovery below Norman castle earthworks at Hen Domen, Montgomeryshire and Sandal Castle, Yorkshire. Ridge and furrow fields comprise sets of sinuous strips, often in a reversed 'S' shape, set out in blocks organised to provide interconnecting drainage systems. The raised centreline of each strip is termed the 'ridge', whist the dips between individual strips are called 'furrows'. The curious form of these strips is the product of a ploughing technique whereby one side of the ridge is ploughed, followed by the other on return. The turning of the plough-team at the ends of strips can lead to the formation of a substantial bank, or 'headland'.

From the late ninth century Anglo-Saxon charter bounds record various features, including 'acres' and 'headlands', which, as Della Hooke has observed, corresponds, with the earlier stages of the process of estate fragmentation. Blocks of strips were divided up amongst the villagers in varying quantity, but the lord of the manor farmed the larger share. The language of the charters that mention field systems is unambiguous in many cases and has recently been reviewed by Hooke. A charter of 963 for Avon in Durnford, Wiltshire, for example, records 'single acres dispersed in a mixture here and there in common land'.

The open field system did not become universally adopted and its heartland remained the midland counties throughout the medieval period. The move toward nucleation suggests a need for greater returns from agricultural yields. The increasing tax burdens of the Late Anglo-Saxon period, including those necessary to fund the substantial payments of coin made to the Vikings (Danegeld), may have resulted in a move toward increased productivity on a scale that had never before been required.

The Anglo-Saxon rural economy, however, was based upon much more than agriculture. Enclosure ditches within settlements indicate not only the development of property rights, but also the need to control animals within the settlement space. Only rarely did the Anglo-Saxons share accommodation with their stock, as at Mawgan Porth, so the maintenance of stock enclosures was surely crucial to the smooth running of an estate centre. Fish-traps, water mills, saltworking sites and looms were the occupational preserve of the lower classes, whilst precious metal workshops, bell-casting pits and glass furnaces are known from high-status sites indicating royal control over production as well as consumption.

Discussion

Clearly, a range of settlement and building types can be observed throughout our period. The availability of building materials and other economic concerns has influenced the architecture and layout of individual sites, although there are some common characteristics such as the basic layout of domestic buildings with their opposing doorways. Overall, the main factor to bear in mind is that of regional variation in settlement type, but variation within the morphology of individual sites is also a notable feature of the settlements of our period.

A very special settlement form is the subject of the following chapter. Certain locations came to possess a number and range of attributes sufficient to ensure their divergence from the common rural model of settlement and these are explored below.

5 Marketing, manufacture and trade: the development of towns

Introduction

A classical concept of urbanism has dominated studies of urban development, but the origins and growth of Anglo-Saxon towns differed greatly from that of their Roman predecessors. It is now firmly established that the towns of Roman Britain had entered a period of terminal decline from at least the third century, with evidence for the decline of major public buildings from the late second century in certain towns such as London. For many years archaeologists sought for evidence for continuity of occupation in the former Roman centres but there has been much debate about what constitutes an urban place in both historical and archaeological terms and this issue is given further consideration below. Roman towns were imposed on a landscape with an existing network of ranked settlements indicating a highly successful economy based upon agricultural production. In direct contrast, Anglo-Saxon towns represent a more organic form of urban development based upon responses to economic and social needs.

Prior to the Second World War, very little archaeological work had taken place in towns. In response to post-war urban redevelopment, however, archaeologists such as W.F. Grimes working in London, attempted to record medieval sites with a vigour and attention to detail only normally associated with Roman remains. Grimes, for example, was to conduct one of the earliest investigations of an urban parish church on a major scale at St Bride's, Fleet Street. Research excavations by Martin Biddle at Winchester in the 1960s and 1970s showed in an impressive fashion how a carefully co-ordinated programme of archaeological work could elucidate the early history of a large town in a fundamental way. More recently, the building boom during the 1980s and the early 1990s has generated a vast new archive of information about urban development, much of which still lies largely untapped.

In the early days of urban studies, the focus of attention was directed toward the understanding of our major towns including London, York, Canterbury, Oxford and Norwich among others. Such an approach, whilst providing valuable information about important regional centres, tended to neglect the smaller towns of Anglo-Saxon England which would have been more familiar to the greater mass of the population, certainly by the tenth century.

This chapter, therefore, explores some aspects of urban development in England with reference to a range of different types of settlements that are broadly grouped under the umbrella of the term 'town'. To begin with though, it is important to consider definitions.

Defining urban status

A number of theories have been advanced in attempts to define both the catalyst(s) and the physical appearance of early towns. Historians such as Maurice Beresford have argued for a definition of urban status largely from a legal perspective, but most now accept that documents such as market charters were often granted retrospectively by kings attempting to rake in taxes from illicit or long established folk markets. Beresford's list further included the presence of burgage plots (rented plots) and other administrative qualifications such as separate taxation arrangements and the existence of a member of a medieval parliament.

Of course, the increased documentary survivals of the post-conquest period throw far more light on the intricacies of urban affairs, but we should not assume that the same criteria could be applied at an earlier period. In fact, archaeologists have probably made the greatest advances in the study of the earlier medieval period in the area of urban development. This situation has led to an increasing desire to define urban status with regard to archaeological evidence first and foremost. In particular, the genesis of expansive settlements performing a range of functions has been almost completely visualised through archaeological research at Southampton, London, Ipswich and York. It is in these towns that the identification and elucidation of Middle Saxon settlements of exceptional character has allowed light to be thrown on the small number of often vague textual references to early trading centres in England. These settlements, known as '*wics*' are considered in further detail below.

Archaeological excavation and topographical studies based on the earliest surviving maps can often provide clues about the broader pattern of developments within towns and a range of such characteristics were listed by Martin Biddle in his pioneering essay on Anglo-Saxon towns published in 1976. Biddle's list included 12 attributes of which the possession of two or more, it is argued, would allow qualification for urban status. These are:

Defences	A relatively large and dense population
A planned street system	A diversified economic base
A market	Plots and houses of urban type
A mint	Social differentiation
Legal autonomy	Complex religious organisation
A role as a central place	A judicial centre

Archaeology is able to illuminate all of these aspects, with the exception of legal autonomy and judicial authority which rely on historical sources to confirm such a role.

More recent approaches to the complexities of urban development have suggested that the search for a clear-cut definition is inappropriate. David Hill has noted that since Sir Frank Stenton defined an Anglo-Saxon town as place with a wall, a mint and a market, scholars have attempted to establish a definition of urban places that could include all types of towns at different stages of their development. It has been further suggested that the search for an all-encompassing description would have been equally as elusive to the Anglo-Saxons as to modern students. Overall, it seems that rather simpler schemes of classification are better suited to the nature of the evidence for complex settlements, from both archaeological and historical sources. Susan Reynolds has provided perhaps the simplest definition of a town, as a settlement where the majority of its inhabitants support themselves through non-agricultural means, whilst Patrick Ottaway has noted Fernand Braudel's statement that: 'the town stood, above all, for domination and what matters most when we try to define or rank it, is the capacity to command and the area it commanded'.

In purely archaeological terms, certain characteristics of archaeological deposits can be used independently or in the absence of historical evidence, to suggest the special character of a given place. The nature of continual deposition on sites densely occupied over a long period is entirely different to that found on rural sites where, as we have noted above, archaeological stratigraphy is often limited to the layers contained within individual post-holes, ditches and pits.

The latter category of features, pits, can be used to suggest a different form of tenurial arrangement from communities which did not use such features. Rural populations, whose livelihood depended on agricultural productivity and the communal organisation of labour, had free access to agricultural land upon which domestic waste was spread, partly to fertilise the soil, partly to keep settlement areas clear of rubbish and rodents. The presence of pits within urban sites implies that the occupants of individual plots were restricted in all aspects of their existence to their rented burgages. Pits served as cesspits and rubbish pits and they indicate just how different the lifestyles of the Anglo-Saxon rural and urban dwellers were in terms of access to space.

Without the aid of documentary sources then, it is possible to identify archaeological deposits that suggest occupation of an entirely different nature from that found on rural sites. In addition to differences in occupation density and modes of waste disposal, the range of local, regional and international imports from an urban site should provide a reflection of the role of that place within local and regional exchange networks. Furthermore, Susan Reynolds' predominantly non-agricultural populations ought to be manifest in a range of specialised crafts and industries, ideally zoned within the urban area.

Differences in housing too can be detected between rural settlements and towns. In the Middle and Late Anglo-Saxon countryside, houses were commonly of simple type with little evidence in most cases for the occupations of their inhabitants. The late seventh century *wics* brought about a new type accommodation, where buildings interpreted as shops lay up against street frontages, with dwelling and workshop space to the rear. By the Late Anglo-Saxon period a distinctive urban type of cellared housing had developed with examples known from Oxford, London, York, Northampton, Thetford and elsewhere. In London, the arrangement of Late Anglo-Saxon houses positioned end on to their street frontages finds parallels elsewhere. This aspect of town planning can only have been employed to maximise the use of space within the town, thus fostering economic prosperity. London's Late Anglo-Saxon timber buildings represent a remarkable exhibition of contemporary carpentry skills through their variety and sophistication. The better quality buildings were built on solid timber sill-beams, whilst others were formed of timber uprights set into the ground with wattle or plank infill.

The development of exceptional central places in Anglo-Saxon England can be divided into three types of sites. The earliest centres to suggest the concentration of formerly dispersed functions are the *wic* sites of late seventh- or early eighth- to ninth-century date. Fortified settlements or burhs have been considered above in terms of their defensive role, but such planned towns seem to have originated in Mercia, perhaps as early as the eighth century; they form a well-defined second group, certainly from the late ninth century. The legislation of the tenth-century West Saxon kings clearly shows how the *burhs* served an important economic role, whilst the presence of minster churches at *burhs* fostered their economic development by attracting pilgrims.

It seems also that of the former Roman towns re-occupied in the earlier part of the Anglo-Saxon period, only those that possessed a minster church flowered as important local and regional centres into later times. John Blair in particular, has argued for the central role of minster churches in the development of smaller towns in England, with the suggestion that they were perhaps more influential than royal estate centres in the early stages of town origins. In a book of this length there is not the space to consider in detail the evidence from the full range of urban excavations undertaken in recent decades. Instead, specific examples are chosen, which illustrate particular points and present rounded case studies.

Wics

The earliest evidence for the development of places serving an exceptional marketing function is found in the form of coastal trading settlements, apparently fostered by the more powerful of the later seventh-century kingdoms. We have considered the near-contemporary late seventh-century laws of Ine of Wessex and Wihtred of Kent in previous chapters, but these codes give an indication of the tightening or formalisation of matters as diverse as the enclosure of personal property to the issue of safe passage along highways. The laws relating to proper use of highways must surely reflect the growing concerns of kings with regard to the regulated movement of people and goods.

Whilst these kings, and probably their counterparts in other regions, appear to have mastered the collection of taxes from rural communities, the growth of trade with continental Europe from the later seventh century onward brought about the need to regulate and tax international commerce. The precise origins of the so-called *wic* sites is still obscure, although there are indications at Southampton and Ipswich of small scale settlements prior to the major phases of settlement planning and development. Gustav Milne has suggested that cross-channel trade developed as a result of fishermen increasing their income by bringing goods from the continent. What is clear, however, is that at least three major settlements had developed by the late seventh century or early eighth century, which were to provide the major kingdoms with international gateways to European trading centres, or emporia, at Quentovic, Dorestadt and Domburg among other places.

The principal English sites are *Hamwic* (Southampton), *Lundenwic* (London) and

73 *Buying and selling at a Middle Anglo-Saxon wic site.* Drawn by Sarah Semple

Gippeswic (Ipswich), although York is a further contender with evidence of eighth- and ninth-century date from the Fishergate excavations. Documentary sources have provided evidence for further *wic* sites in Kent, such as Fordwich and Sandwich, whilst place-names perhaps suggest yet more such sites along the Thames, for example at Greenwich. The archaeological remains from the *wics* so far explored provide a valuable insight to what must have been thriving mercantile centres. The rural *ceorl* could marvel over commodities being unloaded from the ship of a foreign merchant, or those with money to spend could buy something a little more exotic than usual to take home with the shopping (**73**).

The best known of the *wic* sites is Hamwic, located on the west bank of the River Itchen to the south of the Roman fort at *Clausentum* (later the site of the Burghal Hidage fort of *Hamtune*) and to the east of medieval and modern Southampton. The earliest Anglo-Saxon occupation is dated to *c.*700 and the settlement is suggested by some to have developed from a nucleus around the site of St Mary's Church — still the mother church for the city of Southampton. To date, seven cemeteries have been recognised in the area covered by Hamwic and it appears that these burial grounds represent a succession of sites located on the fringes of a rapidly expanding settlement. The maximum extent of the settlement is estimated at between 42 and 52ha. Population estimates are very difficult to make, but a figure of between 2000 and 3000 people at most has been proposed.

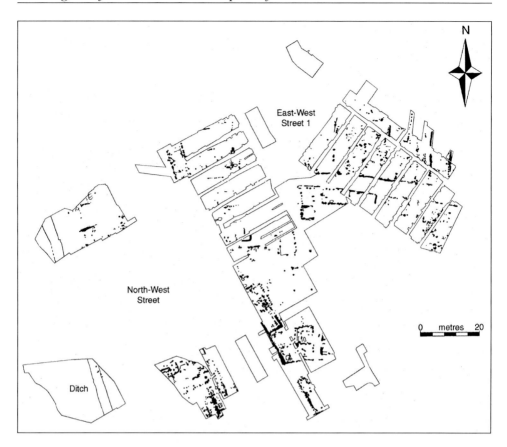

74 *Middle Anglo-Saxon structures at Hamwic (Six Dials), Hampshire. Note the alignments of buildings in relation to the streets (blank areas).* Redrawn from Andrews 1997

Excavations at Hamwic have taken place on a large number of sites, which has allowed archaeologists to piece together information about the layout of streets and houses and the arrangement of properties in relation to each other. Rather than attempting to review the evidence each of the excavated sites, the principal features of one of the most intensively explored areas will be outlined. Excavations were carried out in the area of the town known as Six Dials between 1977 and 1989. The location of the Six Dials site gives some impression of the scale of the Middle Anglo-Saxon trading settlement as it lies on the north-western edge of Hamwic, some 700m from the suggested location of the contemporary waterfront. Besides the impressive remains of some 68 houses and workshops (**74**), 21 wells and 500 pits (**colour plate 17**), the course of a boundary ditch delimiting the western side of the settlement was also found. The ditch measured 3m in width and 1.5m in depth where it ran through the area of the Six Dials intervention, although there is general agreement that the feature did not serve a defensive function. With reference to all of the known *wic* sites, Peter Sawyer notes that 'these places were protected not by physical defences but by the peace of the king'.

75 *A reconstruction of the street pattern of Middle Anglo-Saxon Hamwic.* Redrawn from Andrews 1997

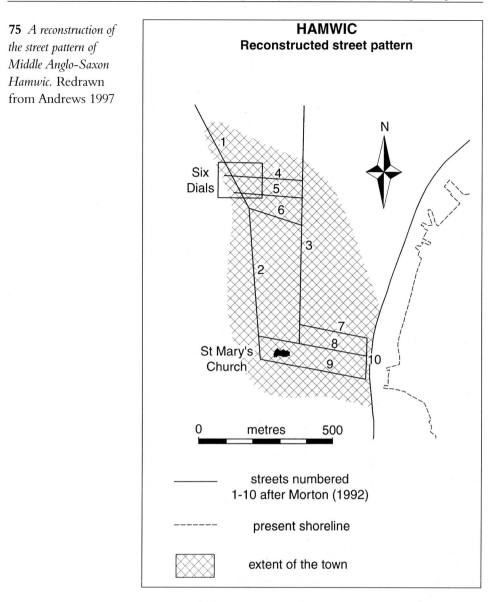

The sequence of events at Six Dials suggests that the ditch was laid out very shortly after Hamwic's principal north-south street, but before the laying out of houses and properties; a sequence that is strikingly comparable with the setting out and building of a modern housing estate. Hamwic's western boundary ditch was to become infilled by the middle of the eighth century, when further expansion occurred westwards.

Centralised planning is evident in the nature of the streets excavated at Hamwic (**75**). Besides their regular gridded layout, streets were resurfaced at regular intervals which has resulted in a stratified build up of surfaces (**76**) providing the type of archaeological deposit one might use to begin to distinguish between a rural and an urban settlement. The main north-south street was about 14m wide, whilst side streets were narrower at about 3m in

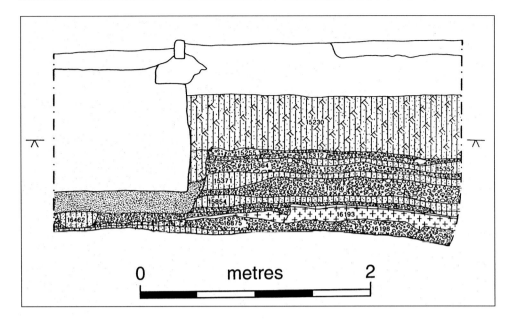

76 *Section drawing of successive street levels at Hamwic (Six Dials).* Redrawn from Andrews 1997

width. As one might expect, the main thoroughfare was re-surfaced more frequently than the minor roads.

Differences between the structures found at Hamwic and those from contemporary rural sites have been noted above, but there are some further observations that can usefully be made. Richard Hodges has noted that the Hamwic buildings are generally less competently erected than their rural counterparts, with less concern for the rigid alignment of post-holes. This aspect has been attributed to the use of unseasoned timber or inexperience on the part of the builders. Most of the structures fall within a size range of 12m in length and 5m in width. Structures were set within properties whose limits can be reconstructed by an analysis of the alignments of pits and stakeholes. In fact, much of the evidence for divisions between individual properties is derived from what archaeologists term 'negative evidence'.

Wells (**colour plate 19**) and rubbish pits (**colour plate 20**) and lay within individual properties, although wells tended to be located either on or close to suggested plot boundaries (**77**). The Six Dials area contained a density of pits twice that of other excavated sites at Hamwic, although this aspect can be explained in terms of a greater density of occupation over a long period. Hamwic's pits contained a wealth of information from which a reconstruction of the economic role of the site could be attempted. Work on the animal and plant remains from the various sites indicates a broadly based economy.

Animals represented by the faunal remains include red and roe deer, although the absence of body parts other than the skull and antlers suggests the supply of raw materials to craft workers. Goat remains were generally rare and mostly limited to sawn horn cores,

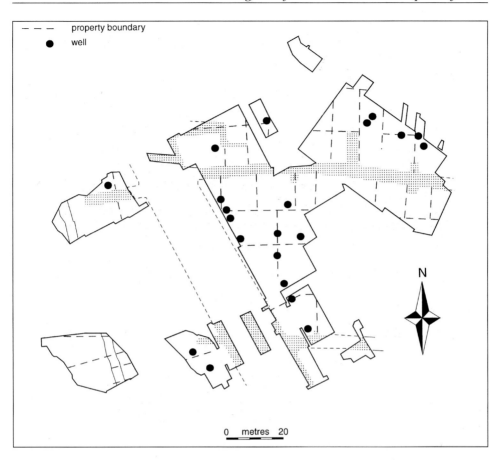

- − − − property boundary
- ● well

0 metres 20

77 *The distribution of wells in relation to property boundaries and streets at Hamwic (Six Dials).* Redrawn from Andrews 1997

again it seems that craftworkers were receiving roughly prepared materials, probably from outside of Hamwic itself. Goose and domestic fowl were evident in the contents of the majority of pits, whilst eel, flatfish and bass indicate local estuarine fishing. Mackerel, conger eel and sea bream provide evidence for fishing in deeper waters. The majority of the animal remains, however, comprised cow (53.5%), sheep (32.1%) and pig (14.4%).

Plotting of the waste materials from craft and industrial activities has allowed a picture of the distribution of various trades to be observed (**78**). In many cases the industries are related in the sense that the either the waste material or the finished product of one industry is necessary for the continuation of another. Perhaps the best example of such an economic process is provided the range of activities associated with animal remains. It appears that basic processing of hides, for example, was undertaken by one establishment, whilst finished products were provided by another. Iron working, along with hide preparation seems to have been undertaken, understandably, in specific structures, whereas other crafts were practised within an otherwise domestic environment.

Although the role of Hamwic in the economy of its local and regional hinterland was

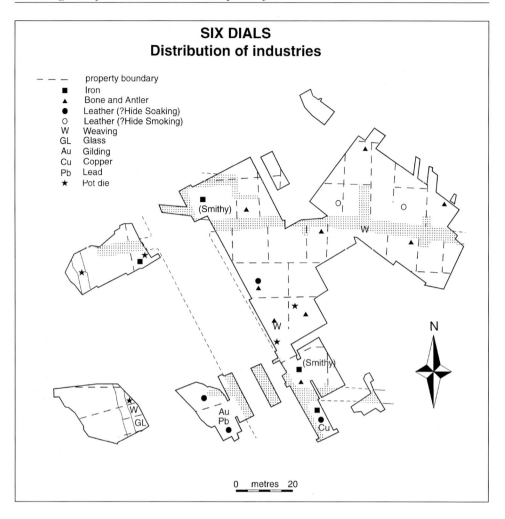

SIX DIALS
Distribution of industries

– – – property boundary
■ Iron
▲ Bone and Antler
● Leather (?Hide Soaking)
○ Leather (?Hide Smoking)
W Weaving
GL Glass
Au Gilding
Cu Copper
Pb Lead
★ Pot die

0 metres 20

78 *The distribution of evidence for craftworking and industry at Hamwic (Six Dials).* Redrawn from Andrews 1997

probably considerable, the evidence for international trade places the site within a firmly European economic context. Finds of imported pottery and coins have allowed Richard Hodges and others to reconstruct trading patterns in north-western Europe on a scale which historical documentation simply will not allow. Imported ceramics are derived mainly from northern France, but significant links with the Rhineland and the Low Countries are also evidenced. The range of continental contacts indicated by the pottery is widened by the geological provenance of millstones and hones in addition to fragments of vessel glass.

As a final indicator of the role of Hamwic in both regional and international trade, a brief note on the coinage from the site is necessary. A wide variety of silver coins known as *sceattas* has been found at Hamwic, with many of the coins recovered from pits. In the usual fashion, only half of the filling of each pit was excavated and, as most of Hamwic's coins were recovered from such contexts it is likely that the number of individual finds is much higher than the known total of about 150. At Six Dials 101 coins were found, of which 70 were Middle Anglo-Saxon *sceattas* or pennies. In addition to the Anglo-Saxon coins, a number of the *sceattas* were probably minted on the continent as poor copies of English exemplars. Of particular interest is a group of sceattas whose distribution is almost entirely restricted to the confines of the Hamwic settlement. The so-called Series H *sceattas*, Types 39, 48 and 49, have fuelled intense debate among numismatists and archaeologists owing to the peculiarities of their distributions. Types 39 and 49 occur almost without exception within the settlement itself. This aspect suggests that Hamwic functioned as a mint, at least during the second and third decades of the eighth century when these types are believed to have been manufactured. Type 48, on the other hand, occurs largely outside Hamwic and some have argued for a different place of origin. An interesting component of the coin assemblage is the presence of 18 Roman coins, apparently selected for their small size either as some form of token or for use as weights.

By 900 occupation of the site of Hamwic was greatly reduced if not completely at an end. It is generally argued that the rise of Winchester during the second half of the ninth century, coupled with changes in the pan-European economic scene and the effects of Viking raiding, ensured that Hamwic was not to become the focus for Late Anglo-Saxon and medieval developments. Indeed, the site of what was to become the great medieval town of Southampton began as a modest ditched enclosure located away from the site of the former *wic*.

The relocation of such a major settlement from its Middle Anglo-Saxon focus around the minster church of St Mary to a separate site is paralleled at London. Here, the *wic* settlement was moved from its site west of the Roman walled town to within it during the late ninth or early tenth centuries, after which time the town became known as *Lundenburh*.

The Middle Anglo-Saxon trading settlement at London is estimated to cover some 55 to 60ha, although its layout and development are less well understood than at other similar sites. Large-scale excavations have recently added to the picture but remain to be fully published in due course.

Early medieval settlement at Ipswich began in the earlier part of the seventh century and comprised an area of some 15 acres (6ha) with an adjacent cemetery, waterfront and pottery industry to the north east of the settlement complex. The settlement expanded massively at a later date to cover an area of about 125 acres (50ha) on both sides of the River Gipping. This phase of expansion was long thought to belong to the early ninth century. The results of a new high-precision radiocarbon dating programme by Christopher Scull and Alex Bayliss, however, have suggested that a cemetery associated with the earliest phase of Ipswich went out of use by the end of the seventh century when the area became engulfed by urban expansion. Regular metalled streets were laid, one of which ran over the former cemetery, with buildings set out along the street frontage. Evidence for production other than pottery was recovered in the form of antler-working and metalworking. Imports of Frankish pottery in particular have been found in sizeable quantities demonstrating the link with continental Europe.

Although Ipswich can be seen to have developed from early in the seventh century, finds indicative of market activity elsewhere in East Anglia suggest a more complex pattern of regional economics at this time.

Rural fairs and other markets

In recent years, the increasing use of metal detectors in East Anglia and Lincolnshire in particular, has brought to light a vast quantity of metal finds, many from sites with no known documented associations. Anglo-Saxon *sceattas* (**colour plate 21**) are often found in significant quantities along with silver strap-ends and other dress fittings of both precious and non-precious metal. These so-called 'productive sites', it is argued, represent the locations of marketing activity of the Middle Anglo-Saxon period. Several such locales are now known, including Barham, Suffolk and Middle Harling, Norfolk, although it is equally possible that such finds represent ploughed residences of Flixborough type.

Besides commercial activity in towns, buying and selling is likely to have occurred at a wide range of different sites wherever people gathered in sufficient numbers. Locations where public gatherings took place on known days would surely have attracted the greater number of merchants and others with goods to sell. With this observation in mind, there is supporting archaeological evidence from an increasing number of church sites for coin loss indicative of marketing. Domesday Book records the presence of markets at a number of important churches that were of minster status in the Middle to Late Anglo-Saxon period. This latter group includes Bampton, Oxfordshire, Oundle, Northamptonshire and Leighton Buzzard and Luton in Bedfordshire.

An obvious context for marketing activity is provided by the regular meetings of the hundred court, whilst the twice-yearly occasion of the shire court must have acted as a magnet to a whole host of 'service providers' — from the Anglo-Saxon equivalent of hotdog stalls to those selling dress fittings and other commodities. In fact, it is difficult to think of a more captive market representing such a broad social spectrum than those in attendance at a hundred meeting.

Small towns

Much less is known about the origins and development of smaller towns, at least from an archaeological perspective. Archaeologists are now beginning to turn their attentions to such places, and pioneering studies include those undertaken by Mark Gardiner at Steyning in West Sussex and by John Blair at Bampton in Oxfordshire. Some aspects of Steyning's development will serve to illustrate the differences between the archaeology of large towns and those of their lesser counterparts.

Steyning (a small town by an historians definition, at least by the time of Domesday) is one of the most intensively excavated and researched of English small towns (**79**). The settlement was clearly important by the middle of the ninth century when King Alfred's father, King Æthelwulf was buried there in 858, only to be moved later to Winchester. The presence of an Anglo-Saxon minster church, purportedly containing the relics of one St

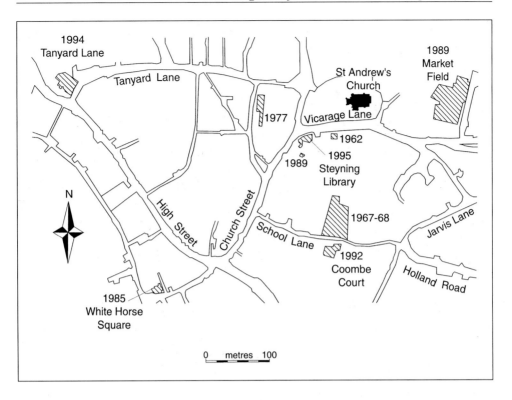

79 *The Late Anglo-Saxon and Medieval Town of Steyning, West Sussex, one of England's most intensively investigated small towns. The extent of the Anglo-Saxon town ran from Tanyard Lane Stream at the north-western edge of the settlement, eastward to Market Field and   southward from the area around St Andrew's Church almost as far as the Medieval High Street.* Redrawn from Gardiner and Greatorex 1997

Cuthman, and the close proximity of the navigable River Adur provide a context for the growth of mercantile activity. By the Late Anglo-Saxon period Steyning was in fact known as the port of St Cuthman; a scenario borne out by the finding of a few continental imports of either Pingsdorf or Beauvais ware from several of the excavations in the town. In 1066 there were 118 houses of note and by 1086 there were 123, with an estimated population of about 600. The finding in 1989 of a Late Anglo-Saxon pewter disc brooch (**80**), of a type associated with urban markets, and coins of King Edgar further support interpretation of the settlement as a market town.

Excavations to the north-east of the rededicated St Andrew's Church in 1989–90 revealed a large part of an enclosed settlement dated to the tenth and eleventh centuries (**81**). The eastern part of what must have been a very large enclosure was found, with a gateway of a type which Mark Gardiner has shown to be a characteristic feature of Late Anglo-Saxon settlements by comparison with examples from Little Paxton, Cambridgeshire and Cheddar (see Chapter 4). Within the enclosure lay two post-built timber buildings of a type common to rural settlement, although the lack of internal

80 *A Late Anglo-Saxon pewter disc brooch from Steyning. Pewter brooches and other trinkets were produced for sale in urban markets and represent the cheaper end of the range of dress accessories. Actual size 28.5mm diameter.* Taken from Reynolds 1994

boundaries within the site gave no indications of formal planning. Groups of pits were associated particularly with Building A (**colour plate 22**), which displayed a higher standard of architecture in its southern end wall than the other structure found on the site, Building B, by the use of carefully prepared, radially-split planks set into stone-packed postholes (**colour plate 23**). The range of ceramics was largely of local manufacture, although the finding of an inscribed gold ring of later ninth-century date, albeit in an eleventh-century context, suggests a high-status owner or perhaps the last keeper of an heirloom (**colour plate 24**).

The layout of the Steyning settlement does not agree with what one might expect to find in a settlement defined in historical terms as a town. The impression is instead one of loosely grouped farmsteads with, in the case of the excavated site, indications of autonomy within enclosed units.

Excavations at other locations within the town broadly confirm the extent of occupation during the Late Anglo-Saxon period. The layout of properties on the north-east side of the clearly planned medieval High Street suggests the former existence of enclosures of Market Field type between the new development and the former Anglo-Saxon minster church. Trial excavations to the north of the church have failed to produce evidence for occupation during the Anglo-Saxon period. Excavations to the south and west of the church indicate that not all of the area occupied by the settlement was covered with buildings. In fact, the density of occupation appears to have been rather low by comparison to the better-known larger towns of the period. On the basis of observations at the Market Field site, it appears that Anglo-Saxon Steyning was characterised by a loose agglomeration of enclosures containing buildings. Whilst pits found in the larger towns

81 *The Late Anglo-Saxon settlement at Market Field, Steyning. Note the boundary ditches and gateway and the clustering of refuse pits at either end of Building A. R*edrawn from Gardiner 1993

are generally distributed throughout individual plots, at Steyning there is a tendency for rubbish disposal to occur in close proximity to dwellings despite the fact that pressure on land appears rather less of a problem than in the large towns. The cesspits at Market Field were located away from the excavated buildings.

Mark Gardiner has suggested that there was little to distinguish the pre-conquest residents of Steyning from their 'rural' counterparts, noting that Domesday Book refers to the burgesses' (tenants) working 'at court like villans'. In other words, the occupants of the Late Anglo-Saxon town were labelled as town dwellers according to traditional historical definition, but the reality of their lives was hard to distinguish from that of the rural farmer.

A range of economic activities have been identified within the Late Anglo-Saxon town

173

including iron-working. The majority of the evidence for production, however, comprises agricultural produce. A careful examination of samples of soil from various ditches and pits identified wheat, barley, flax and perhaps oats, beans and vetch. Wild foods formed an important part of the diet and included apples, sloes, plums, rose-hips and hazelnuts, although it is always possible that such commodities were sold at market by enterprising individuals rather than personally gathered by the owners of the Market Field settlement.

Larger Late Anglo-Saxon towns

In contrast to the evidence for the development of small towns, the work of urban archaeologists in the larger centres has enabled a much clearer picture to emerge of the nature of urban life in the larger towns. As with previous topics, there is not the space to consider the contribution made to urban studies by archaeologists working in each of the major towns, instead some general observations will be made before turning to the extensive work done in Norwich as a case study.

After the heyday of the *wic*-type settlements had passed, urban regeneration began with the programme of burghal town planning discussed in Chapter 3. We have already considered Winchester's streets in that discussion, but other towns were furnished with equally impressive townscapes. In London, a central core of streets was laid out during the reign of Alfred, which marked the beginning of mercantile activity within the walled city after a break of 500 years (**82**). As David Hill has shown, the legislation of the West Saxon kings contains much of interest with regard to changes in marketing activity. King Alfred's laws requiring traders to report to the king's reeve at a public assembly suggest that markets were dispersed widely and that transactions took place at public meetings. Edward the Elder, in his first law code states that 'every man shall have a warrantor [to his transactions] and that no-one shall buy [and sell] except in a market town; but he shall have the witness of the 'port-reeve' or of other men of credit, who can be trusted'. During the period from the late ninth to the middle of the tenth century, therefore, towns came to occupy, as Hill notes, 'a monopoly position'. This monopoly was further strengthened during the reign of Athelstan who legislated with regard to the centralisation of ecclesiastical and secular administration within towns including the minting of coins. The later tenth-century kings did much to encourage urban development, perhaps most striking of all was King Edgar's reform of the coinage which required the regular recalling of silver pennies for re-minting. The crown benefited by the levying of a tax each time the coinage was recalled.

The burghal towns of Wessex and Mercia present topographical characteristics that belie their planned origins. An example of a town that grew in a more organic fashion is Norwich (**83**). Late Anglo-Saxon Norwich developed in rather different ways from the *wics* and *burhs*. Instead of evolving from a single nucleus, it appears that Middle Anglo-Saxon Norwich was formed of several settlements that eventually coalesced to form a large sprawling town by the time of the Norman Conquest. Coins of *c.*900 are known bearing a Norwich mint-signature, but the documentary record is sparse prior to the twelfth century. A valuable piece of information is provided by the *Anglo-Saxon Chronicle* entry for 1004, which records how 'Swein came with his fleet to Norwich, and completely

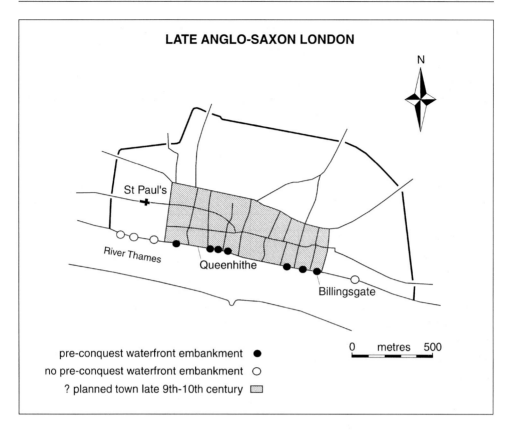

82 *London in the Late Anglo-Saxon period. The central core or streets was most likely laid out during the reign of Alfred after his capture of the city in AD 886.* Redrawn from Milne and Goodburn 1990

raided and burned down the town'. The nature of the town referred to at this time has taken considerable efforts to understand. It now seems that the disparate settlements established in the eighth and ninth centuries, expanded organically until the tenth century by which time Norwich can be considered a full blown town. Despite rapid urban growth, Norwich appears to have retained open areas within the limits of the town throughout its life.

The location of the principal settlement focus has proved difficult to pin down. Prior to the 1985 excavations at Fishergate on the north bank of the River Wensum, it was believed that the early core of the settlement lay to the south of the river in the vicinity of the cathedral close within a large ditched enclosure. The Fishergate exploration, however, lay just to the east of Fyebridge, within an area later described by a further ditched enclosure of probable tenth-century date. The site revealed the largest concentration of Middle Anglo-Saxon material recovered from any single excavation within the city. Unfortunately the Middle Anglo-Saxon finds were mixed in with later deposits, although it seems likely that these represent the refuse generated by early properties close to the river bank. After

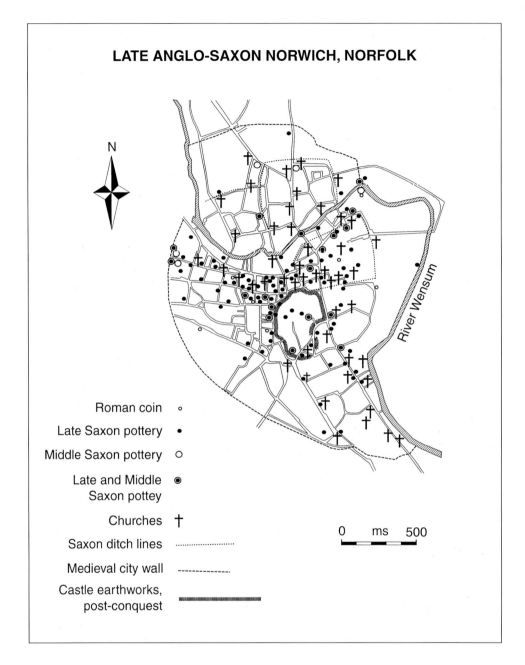

LATE ANGLO-SAXON NORWICH, NORFOLK

N

River Wensum

Roman coin	∘
Late Saxon pottery	•
Middle Saxon pottery	○
Late and Middle Saxon pottey	◉
Churches	†
Saxon ditch lines	··········
Medieval city wall	-------
Castle earthworks, post-conquest	▓▓▓▓▓▓▓

0   ms   500

83 *Late Anglo-Saxon Norwich. By plotting finds of Late Anglo-Saxon date, it is possible to reconstruct the extent of the town prior to the Norman Conquest. The irregular street pattern belies the organic development of the town, which possessed about 50 churches by the time of the Domesday Survey.* Redrawn from Campbell 1982

the re-conquest of the eastern Danelaw in 917, Norwich served as an administrative centre, although this function may well have originated during the period of Viking control from *c*.870–*c*.917. From the middle of the eleventh century onward the city has been largely concentrated to the south of the river, possibly as a result of Swein's attack on the settlement and the subsequent redevelopment that occurred.

By the time of the Domesday Survey, the population of Norwich was probably in excess of 5000 people, which is closely comparable with estimates for Winchester and Lincoln at this time. Economic prosperity during the tenth and eleventh centuries is reflected by the foundation of many new churches within the town. By the time of the Domesday Survey there were at least 46 parish churches. The appearance of such a large number of churches on urban estates in the century before the Norman conquest is, of course, paralleled in the countryside as we have seen in Chapter 4. Besides Norwich's marketing functions, the production of pottery, particularly on the western side of the town appears to have been an important industry. Perhaps the activities of potters were limited to parts of the town where there was less chance of setting fire to domestic buildings. Indeed, the effectiveness of fire as a means of levelling Late Anglo-Saxon towns was clearly appreciated by the Vikings.

Organic urban development, such as that observed at Norwich, can be seen at other Late Anglo-Saxon towns such as Oxford and Winchester, where suburbs had developed prior to the Norman Conquest. At Oxford, suburbs had developed on all four sides of the *burh* by *c*.1000, and at Winchester the town expanded westward outside the walls. Some idea of the commercial specialisation of particular areas within the Late Anglo-Saxon town, can be inferred from the study of street-names. Unfortunately, most street names are of relatively recent origin, but there are medieval survivals that might relate in origin to the zoning of mercantile activities in the Late Anglo-Saxon period. As a final point, the presence of waterfront structures in towns can give some indication of the size of vessels engaging in the loading and unloading of cargoes.

Discussion

A ranked system of markets can be seen to have operated in both Middle and Late Anglo-Saxon England. The late seventh- to mid-ninth-century *wics* served as key trading centres, although markets based on minster churches or royal estate centres most likely represented the normal shopping experience for the mass of the population. From the seeds sown in the late ninth century in Wessex, in the form of the burghal towns, and in the Danelaw, by the foundation of the Danish boroughs, urbanism developed at a remarkable pace. It is a sobering observation, albeit crude, that by the time of the Norman Conquest England possessed about twice as many places that could be described as towns than it did during the height of town life in Roman Britain.

The concentration of functions that most towns possessed by the middle of the eleventh century included many of those on Biddle's list, including, in certain cases, judicial authority in the form of hundredal courts that had moved from their ancient sites to the protection of the town. In fact, all of the functions that can be found in the towns of the Late Anglo-Saxon period existed during the Middle Anglo-Saxon period, but they

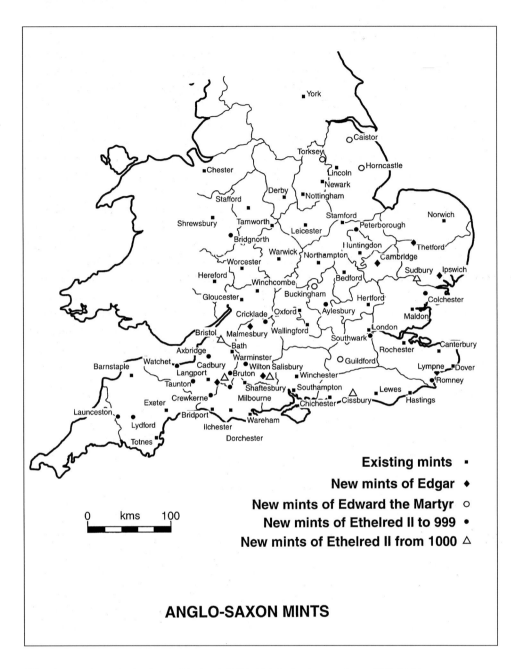

84 *Mints in Late Anglo-Saxon England (957-1016).* Redrawn from Hill 1981

were dispersed throughout discreet territories — the precursors to the units explicitly termed hundreds by the tenth century. This observation is important for it further plays down the classical approach to settlement studies, which considers the city as the ultimate settlement type. Middle Anglo-Saxon England, by contrast, possessed only a small handful of places which might be classed as towns, yet by the ninth century, it supported a monetary economy, systems of taxation and of law and order, and the capability to enact civil works, sometimes on an extraordinary scale — as represented by Offa's Dyke. The even distribution of mints and the coinage reforms of the Late Anglo-Saxon period are a remarkable testimony to the efficiency with which the royal administrative machine attempted to run the national economy (**84**).

Developments in the towns are reflected by changes in the geography and exploitation of the countryside. The network of *herepað* routes, maintained principally for military purposes was expanded during the Late Anglo-Saxon period with the laying of new routes and the renaming of old ones as 'portway' (meaning 'market way'). Good overland communications were an essential component of both economic and defensive networks (**colour plate 25**). The commercial growth witnessed in the towns of the Late Anglo-Saxon period is paralleled in the countryside by the appearance of open field agriculture in many regions. Both urban and rural developments, therefore, require consideration alongside each other for the fullest picture of the period to be drawn.

Postscript — Anglo-Saxon England after the Norman Conquest

The Norman Conquest has long held a special place in English history. The emphasis on the moment of Conquest itself however, has resulted in a rather misleading impression of the overall effects of this event. The Norman takeover, although politically devastating for the English aristocracy, seemingly had little effect on much of the rural scene. Certainly, English landowners were dispossessed of their holdings on a monumental scale but there are, nevertheless, a significant number of English landowners named in 1086 in the Domesday Survey. It is also probable that the English descent of many of the landowners and farmers recorded in twelfth-century sources is disguised by the Norman personal names that became increasingly popular during that century. Furthermore, Anglo-Saxon England continued to function in terms of law, governance and aspects of material culture into the twelfth century.

In cultural terms there is little trace in the archaeological record for the emergence of a new elite. Castles are often cited as one of the principal indicators of the arrival of new overlords, but as we have seen in Chapter 3, fortified towers at least would have been a common sight in mid-eleventh-century England. The appearance of castles certainly marks a departure in terms of the architectural repertoire of the eleventh century, but many of the earliest castles were relatively small and lacked complex architecture. It is the positioning of castles in the landscape that suggests a break with the old order. Early Norman castles founded in Late Anglo-Saxon towns were often sited with a total disregard for existing topography. This aspect is clearly shown at Oxford where excavations under the castle mound revealed pits dating to the Late Anglo-Saxon period. Besides illustrating a disregard for existing occupants of properties, the urban castle builders were providing their masters with a style of fortification that differed greatly from that familiar to the Late Anglo-Saxons. Instead of operating a public system of defence, Norman strongholds were private residences. The imposition of the castle into the English landscape represents not only a disregard for existing tenurial arrangements, especially in the towns, but further served to emphasise the nature of social class distinction by the fact that the residences of the new elite were physically elevated above the vanquished natives. The Tower of London serves as a perfect example of this sort of process, sited as it is so that continental traffic entering the Thames Estuary and travelling down to the port of London could not have failed to note the location of the new royal headquarters. In fact, the Normans built castles in association with administrative centres at a number of other towns, often within a short time of the conquest, with examples at Lincoln, Nottingham, Thetford and Warwick.

Castle building could also have indirect effects. At Bramber Castle in West Sussex, just to the south of the town of Steyning considered in Chapter 5, the building of a bridge there effectively put an end to the passage of river traffic to the former port of Steyning thus emphasising the power of the nearby lord.

The agricultural landscape remained almost wholly unchanged. Although the rural landscape exhibits an added layer of agricultural exploitation, in the form of rabbit warrens and windmills, these are not immediate developments at the time of the conquest. The open field system of farming was at an advanced stage of development and well suited to the feudal organisation of the new regime. Material culture, including dress fashions, ceramics, metal objects and language remained largely unchanged, at least to begin with. Peasant housing remained almost completely unaltered until about 1200 when the long-house tradition, seen earlier at Mawgan Porth, became widespread over England. The nature of rural building techniques too changed around 1200 with a move away from earthfast buildings utilising individual posts set into the ground. Instead new features such as dwarf-walls (low masonry walls which served as a foundation for a timber superstructure) became common. The masonry architecture of the Norman period is outstanding when at its best, for example at Stewkley Church, Buckinghamshire, but it is still representative of the broader Romanesque style of architecture found throughout continental Europe. In fact, the masonry architecture of eleventh-century England is commonly impossible to date to either side of the conquest. The emergence of an insular style of Gothic architecture, known as Early English in the latter part of the twelfth century simply concurs with the dating suggested by other categories of material or architectural culture. Whilst one would not wish to play down the impact of the conquest on peoples lives, there is little indication from archaeological evidence for a major change at about the time of the Norman invasion.

In northern England, resistance to the Normans resulted in a violent suppression that entailed the destruction of many settlements. Life in these regions must have been wholly different to that in southern England where the web of estates and settlements established during the tenth century continued to function without significant disruption. In fact, the reduced values of certain landholdings after the conquest can be viewed through the Domesday Survey, although for the areas hardest hit there are no Domesday records.

Attempting to discern the Norman Conquest in the archaeological record is fraught with problems of establishing what we might expect to find. Dating is a major issue that clouds the picture given the broad dating margins applied to excavated sites of the so-called Saxo-Norman period. This term, in fact, describes a period of English culture that lasted from at least 950 until about 1150 or even 1200.

The extraordinary relationship between society and landscape observed during the Anglo-Saxon period has left its most substantial mark in the countryside. This book, therefore, has attempted to provide an introduction to the Anglo-Saxons and their world and it is hoped that all those who begin to look for their own piece of Anglo-Saxon England will be fittingly rewarded by the discovery of some long-forgotten landscape feature or by the dawning realisation of the significance of a familiar place-name.

Further reading

The guide to further reading presented below is by no means intended as a complete bibliography for the topics and sites addressed by this book. Rather, the intention is to provide pointers to works that either place a subject within a broader historical context or provide model case studies of particular social or economic processes. All of the works cited contain further references that will enable readers to tackle the intricacies of particular problems if required.

Annual bibliographies of works published in all fields of Anglo-Saxon studies are listed in the journal *Anglo-Saxon England*, whilst an extensive mine of references can be found in *Anglo-Saxon History: A Select Bibliography* by S Keynes (University of Cambridge). The journals *Medieval Archaeology* and *Anglo-Saxon Studies in Archaeology and History* are major outlets for academic papers.

Primary sources

S Bradley *Anglo-Saxon Poetry* (London 1995 revised edition).
B Colgrave and R A B Mynors (eds) *Bede's Ecclesiastical History of the English People* (Oxford 1969)
D Douglas and G Greenaway (eds) *English Historical Documents Volume II* (London 1981 second edition)
M Godden and M Lapidge (eds) *The Cambridge Companion to Old English Literature* (Cambridge 1991)
F Harmer *Anglo-Saxon Writs* (Manchester 1952).
P Sawyer *Anglo-Saxon Charters: An Annotated List and Bibliography* (London 1968)
M Swanton *Anglo-Saxon Prose* (London 1993 revised edition)
M Swanton *The Anglo-Saxon Chronicle* (London 1996)
D Whitelock *English Historical Documents Volume I* (London 1979 second edition)
F Attenborough *The Laws of the Earliest English Kings* (Cambridge 1922)
A Robertson *The Laws of the Kings of England from Edmund to Henry I* (Cambridge 1925)

Introduction: sources and approaches

J. Campbell (ed.) *The Anglo-Saxons* (London 1982)
M Gelling *Signposts to the Past* (Chichester 1978)
D Hill An *Atlas of Anglo-Saxon England* (Oxford 1981)
D Hinton *Archaeology, Economy and Society* (London 1990)
R Hodges *The Anglo-Saxon Achievement* (London 1989)

E John *Reassessing Anglo-Saxon England* (Manchester 1996)

B Mitchell *An Invitation to Old English and Anglo-Saxon England* (Oxford 1995)

F Stenton *Anglo-Saxon England* (Oxford 1971 third edition)

D Whitelock *The Beginnings of English Society* (Harmondsworth 1972)

D Wilson (ed.) *The Archaeology of Anglo-Saxon England* (Cambridge 1976)

England in the seventh century and the Early Anglo-Saxons

M Carver *Sutton Hoo Burial Ground of Kings* (London 1998)

H Hamerow *Excavations at Mucking. Volume 2: the Anglo-Saxon Settlement* (London 1993)

J Hines (ed.) *The Anglo-Saxons from the Migration Period to the Eighth Century: an ethnographic perspective* (Woodbridge 1997)

B Hope-Taylor *Yeavering. An Anglo-British Centre of Early Northumbria* (London 1977)

M Welch *English Heritage Book of Anglo-Saxon England* (London 1992)

S West *West Stow, The Anglo-Saxon Village* (East Anglian Archaeology 24, 1985)

The people: social scales and social relationships

H Loyn *The Governance of Anglo-Saxon England* (London 1984)

D Whitelock *The Beginnings of English Society* (Harmondsworth 1972) – chapter 5

The landscape: territorial arrangements and the governance of the realm

S Bassett (ed.) *The Origins of Anglo-Saxon Kingdoms* (Leicester 1989)

J Blair *Anglo-Saxon Oxfordshire* (Stroud 1994)

D Hill paper on Anglo-Saxon beacons in A Rumble and D Mills (eds), *Names, Places and People* (Stamford 1997)

C Hollister *Anglo-Saxon Military Institutions* (Oxford 1962)

D Hooke *The Landscape of Anglo-Saxon England* (Leicester 1998)

H Loyn *The Governance of Anglo-Saxon England 500-1087* (London 1984)

A Meaney paper on hundred meeting-places in A Rumble and D Mills (eds), *Names, Places and People* (Stamford 1997)

D Parsons contribution to a paper on Earl's Barton Anglo-Saxon tower (*Archaeological Journal* 152, 1995)

C Phythian-Adams *Land of the Cumbrians* (Aldershot 1996)

P Sawyer *Anglo-Saxon Lincolnshire* (Lincoln 1998)

P Warner *The Origins of Suffolk* (Manchester 1996)

B Yorke *Wessex in the Early Middle Ages* (Leicester 1995)

The landscape: settlements in the countryside

G Beresford *Goltho: the development of an early medieval Manor c.850-1150* (London 1987)

R Bruce-Mitford *Mawgan Porth. A settlement of the late Saxon period on the north Cornish coast*

(London 1997)

D Coggins, K Fairless and C Batey Simy Folds: An Early Medieval Settlement Site in
	Upper Teesdale (*Medieval Archaeology* 27, 1983)

J Fairbrother Faccombe Netherton. *Excavations of a Saxon and Medieval Manorial Complex*
(British Museum Occasional Paper 74, 1990)

P Fasham, D Farwell and R Whinney *The Archaeological Site at Easton Lane, Winchester*
	(Hampshire Field Club Monograph 6, 1989)

M Faull (ed.) *Studies in Late Anglo-Saxon Settlement* (Oxford 1984)

A Graham and S Davies *Excavations in Trowbridge, Wiltshire, 1977 and 1986-88.* (Wessex
Archaeology Report 2, 1993)

C Loveluck A high-status Anglo-Saxon settlement at Flixborough, Lincolnshire (*Antiquity*
	72, 1998)

G Milne and JD Richards *Two Anglo-Saxon Buildings and Associated Finds* (Wharram A
	Study of Settlement on the Yorkshire Wolds 7, 1992)

P Rahtz *The Saxon and Medieval Palaces at Cheddar* (Oxford 1979)

K Wade paper on Wicken Bonhunt, in D Buckley (ed), *Archaeology in Essex to AD 1500*
	(London 1980)

P Wade-Martins *Excavations in North Elmham Park 1967-1972* (East Anglian Archaeology
9, 1980)

Medieval Archaeology 35 (1991) — a volume of articles on buildings and settlements

Marketing, manufacture and trade: the development of towns

P Andrews *Excavations at Hamwic: Volume 2* (York 1997)

M Biddle paper on Towns in D Wilson (ed.), *The Archaeology of Anglo-Saxon England*
	(Cambridge 1976)

M Carver *Underneath English Towns* (London 1987)

H Clarke and B Ambrosiani Towns in the Viking Age (London 1991)

M Gardiner and C Greatorex Archaeological excavations in Steyning, 1992-95: Further
	evidence for the evolution of a Late Saxon small town (*Sussex Archaeological Collections*
	135, 1997)

D Hill paper on Towns in D Hooke (ed.), *Anglo-Saxon Settlements* (Oxford 1988)

R Hodges *Dark Age Economics* (London 1982)

D Metcalf *An Atlas of Anglo-Saxon and Norman Coin Finds 973-1066* (London 1998)

P Ottaway *Archaeology in British Towns* (London 1992)

C Scull paper on *wics* in J Hines (ed.), *The Anglo-Saxons from the Migration Period to the
	Eighth Century* (Woodbridge 1997)

A Vince *Saxon London* (London 1990)

Postscript — The end of Anglo-Saxon England and the impact of the Norman Conquest

J Campbell (ed.) *The Anglo-Saxons* (London 1982)

H Loyn *Anglo-Saxon England and the Norman Conquest* (London 1991)

Index